THE STORY OF THE OLD TESTAMENT

THE UNIVERSITY OF CHICAGO PRESS
CHICAGO, ILLINOIS

—

THE BAKER & TAYLOR COMPANY
NEW YORK

THE CAMBRIDGE UNIVERSITY PRESS
LONDON

THE MARUZEN-KABUSHIKI-KAISHA
TOKYO, OSAKA, KYOTO, FUKUOKA, SENDAI

THE COMMERCIAL PRESS, LIMITED
SHANGHAI

THE STORY OF
THE OLD TESTAMENT

By

EDGAR J. GOODSPEED

3/802
THE UNIVERSITY OF CHICAGO PRESS
CHICAGO · ILLINOIS

TO

DR. CASSIUS DOUGLAS WESCOTT
IN GRATITUDE AND AFFECTION

INTRODUCTION

The Old Testament is full of dramatic situations and great religious truths, but these are dimly perceived by most people nowadays. Grotesque elements in its art sometimes completely overshadow its most tremendous religious values—as in the story of Jonah. Superficial reading of its books often leaves us with no idea at all of the situations in which they were written and without which they cannot be understood.

For the Old Testament is a very difficult book. It is not easy to recover the occasions on which its great utterances were first formulated or the needs to meet which its books were written. Read solely in the order in which we possess it, the order of its subject matter rather than of its literary origin, it is often very obscure. That orderly corpus of twelve books from Genesis to II Kings is indeed a masterpiece of literary organization, and embodies obvious and indispensable values. But there are in the literature other values less obvious but just as indispensable, which demand another order of treatment to bring them out. For the Hebrew religion did not, after all, begin with the priests but with the prophets, and this fact is reflected in its literature. To follow the emergence of its great ideas as the great literary prophets advanced them one after another gives us a truer and even more dramatic picture of that amazing religious development. Great mountains may be looked at from conventional points of view, as the Jungfrau is from Interlaken, or Mont Blanc from Chamonix, but there are other views of them just as true and just as stupendous.

So it is with the Old Testament. We shall know it better if we study it not simply in the familiar order of its subject matter, but in the order of its origins, of its composition, and of its authors. Great progress has in recent years been made in these directions, and while it is of course impossible to claim unanimity on all points, some things about the writings of the Old Testament have gradually become tolerably clear. The progress of archaeology; the decipherment of Assyrian, Babylonian, and Egyptian remains; and the study of ancient religions have helped immensely to the understanding of the Old Testament.

The task is complicated by the fact that many books of the Old Testament have sustained accretions and undergone revision by later hands. It is as though they had been revised and amplified again and again, and come to us in the last form that they assumed—a sort of final revision. One must choose between dividing their material, taking it up part here and part there, or placing them at a point in history which their major interest, their literary or historical center of gravity, suggests. The former method has often been followed, but seems more likely to confuse than to help the reader.

I have therefore arranged the books in the general order of their composition, realizing that it is difficult to be wholly consistent in any arrangement that refuses to break the books in pieces. It is true, for example, that Jeremiah began to preach before Nahum, but the mass of Jeremiah's work falls after the mass of Nahum's, and Jeremiah can be better understood after Nahum than Nahum after Jeremiah.

It is still true that the *Story of the Old Testament* cannot be written with the same definiteness with which the *Story of the New* can be told. And yet there is room for such a book, as a guide and introduction to the reading and the study of the Old Testament, the great religious values of which are so little appreciated even by intelligent people today. Many problems supposedly quite modern are tellingly dealt with in the Old Testament; indeed, our social reformers are simply saying over again just what the Hebrew prophets said twenty-five hundred years ago. We still need the voice of the prophets. And after all it was they rather than the priests who were the real makers of Israel's religion.

My colleague, Dr. Ernest C. Colwell, has obliged me by reading the book in manuscript, and my brother, Charles T. B. Goodspeed, has very kindly read all the proofs.

EDGAR J. GOODSPEED

UNIVERSITY OF CHICAGO
January 15, 1934

CONTENTS

CHAPTER I

THE BOOK OF AMOS

Jewish literature begins with a plea for justice for the poor. It was made by a poor Hebrew working-man of the eighth century before Christ. His name was Amos. He lived in Tekoa, a village a few miles south of Jerusalem, where he worked as a shepherd and a dresser of sycamore trees.[1]

Long before the time of Amos, the kingdom of David and Solomon had broken into two kingdoms, Israel and Judah, and Amos sometimes found his way up to Bethel, a great sanctuary of the Northern Kingdom, to sell his produce. There, as at Jerusalem itself, he was stirred by the misery of the poor and their oppression by the rich. Even then it was urban life that enhanced these differences and embittered them.

The prophets had fallen into disrepute. They were mercenary and insincere. So when Amos at Bethel burst forth with denunciations of the rich for their selfish cruelty to the poor, and foretold the destruction that such courses would bring upon Israel, the priest Amaziah ordered him off, contemptuously advising him to tell his story in Jerusalem, where reflections on the rival Northern Kingdom would be better received and rewarded. Amos indignantly replied that he was not a prophet nor a member of any prophetic order, but a simple workingman, whom the Lord had taken from following his flock, to send to prophesy to his people Israel. Amos predicts ruin and death for Amaziah, and destruction and exile for the Northern Kingdom.[2]

Amos uttered his prophecies about the middle of the eighth century before Christ, 765–750 B.C., and within a generation the Northern Kingdom fell before the Assyrians under Sargon, who in 721 B.C. carried the inhabitants of Samaria into captivity.[3]

The activity of Amos fell in the reign of Jeroboam II of Israel, 781–740 B.C., for Amaziah reported his seditious utterances to that king.[4] It was a time of political success, for Jeroboam had won back all that the Syrians had taken from the kingdom before his time.[5] With this came material prosperity and its attendant luxury and indulgence. It is against this background of wealth and splendor— ivory houses, palaces of hewn stone, with ivory couches, wine and revelry, lyre and song[6]—that Amos sees in sharp contrast the condition of the poor, set aside and trampled upon by corrupt judges, priests, and nobles, who make the measure small and the price great, and use false scales, so as to sell the innocent for silver and the needy for a pair of sandals;[7] men who are so absorbed in business that they can hardly wait for feast days and Sabbaths to pass, so that they can resume their trade in wheat, though it is only the poorest of it that they will sell to the common people of the land.[8]

Upon all this luxury and exploitation Amos proclaims the judgment of God. Israel has sinned like the nations around, and God will not spare her. Destruction and captivity are to overtake her. The palace songs will become dirges, the shout of the revelers will pass away, the pampered ladies of Samaria, the "cows of Bashan," who oppress the weak and crush the needy, will be dragged forth dead from the city, and thrown unburied on the rubbish heaps.[9] They have treasured up the fruits of violence and robbery in their palaces.[10] But the Assyrians will gather about Samaria and carry her into exile beyond Damascus.[11]

The centers of Israel's hypocritical worship will not be spared.

"The high places of Isaac shall be laid waste;
And the sanctuaries of Israel shall be ruined;
And I will rise against the house of Jeroboam
    with the sword."[12]

Most of Amos' prophecies were directed against Israel. But he looked abroad upon the nations around and saw in each some great sin to condemn, and for every one—Syria, Philistia, Ammon, Moab, Israel—he predicted punishment and overthrow.[13] Amos saw that peace and prosperity have their outrages no less than war, and he denounces the eco-

nomic vices of Israel just as strongly as the more
violent crimes of her neighbors. In this recognition
of God as no mere national deity but as supreme
over the nations and impartial in his judgment upon
them we see for the first time what has been called
the ethical monotheism of the prophets.

Amos saw no hope for the Northern Kingdom.
Its fate was sealed. Such passages in the Book of
Amos as promise restoration are the work of later
hands, through which his writing has passed.[14]

Many things mark this earliest of the literary
prophets with distinction. His lofty idea of God, supreme over the nations and absolutely just; his own
deep moral earnestness, fearlessly assailing the sins
of the rich and privileged of his own nation; his religious insight and his splendid rhetoric mark this
herdsman of Tekoa out in the annals of literature
and of religion.

"The Lord roars from Zion,
  And from Jerusalem he utters his voice"; . . . .
  When the lion roars, who does not fear?
  When the Lord God speaks, who will not
    prophesy?[15]
  He who made the Pleiades and Orion,
  Who turns dense darkness to dawn,
  And darkens day into night.[16]

"Prepare to meet your God, O Israel!"[17] . . . .
  Let justice roll down like waters,
  And righteousness like a perennial stream."[18]

The literature of Western Asia was usually anonymous, growing up as a social product out of many minds, and connected with no individual's name. The great exception is the literary prophets of Judaism. Their utterances were so individual, and so definitely related to specific occasions and situations, that their names were attached to them, and they became the first "authors" of the Bible. Their messages and oracles were usually cast in poetic form so that these early prophets were also poets.

But above all they were the fearless and unsparing critics of the national life and morals. Their poetic and literary gifts were steadily directed to the reformation of their people. Their condemnation was directed not so much at neglect of law or cultus, or what might be called specifically religious duties, but at moral wrong—cruelty, dishonesty, and social injustice. In these they saw the most serious disobedience to the will of God, and against these they waged unceasing war, at no matter what cost to themselves. This is the greatest glory of the Hebrew prophets.

SUGGESTIONS FOR STUDY

1. *References:* [1]Amos 1:1; 7:14; [2]Amos 7:10-17; [3]II Kings 17:4-6; [4]Amos 7:10; [5]II Kings 14:23-25; [6]Amos 3:15; 5:11; 6:4,5; [7]Amos 2:6; [8]Amos 8:5,6; [9]Amos 4:1-3; [10]Amos 3:10; [11]Amos 3:9; 5:27; [12]Amos 7:9; [13]Amos, chap. 1; [14]Amos 9:9-15; [15]Amos 1:2; 3:8; [16]Amos 5:8; [17]Amos 4:12; [18]Amos 5:24.

2. Where did Amos live and what was his occupation?

3. In what literary form did he cast his prophecies?

4. Where did he do most of his prophetic work?

5. What was the political condition of the Kingdom of Israel in his day?

6. What are the sins which Amos especially condemns?

7. What punishment does he threaten Israel with?

8. Relate Amos' interview with Amaziah.

9. What was the current estimate of prophets in his time?

10. What is meant by the ethical monotheism of the prophets?

11. Locate the nations of chapters 1 and 2 on the map.

12. On the oracle against Edom, 2:11, 12, compare Obadiah and its parallels.

13. What became of the Northern Kingdom?

14. What picture of Israelitish civilization appears in Amos?

15. What was the character of the Assyrians?

16. What was the prevailing view of the origin of books in Western Asia?

17. Is there any modern application of the ideas of Amos, or are they obsolete and out of date?

CHAPTER II

THE BOOK OF HOSEA

The prophets taught by deeds as well as words. They dramatized and acted their messages. By their strange and arresting conduct they would attract popular attention to what they wished to convey, and thus impress it deeply upon the public. They did not hesitate to do very sensational things to this end. The most sensational of these prophetic acts was the marriage of Hosea.

Hosea was a prophet of the Northern Kingdom of Israel. He was profoundly convinced that his nation had been unfaithful to God. Israel was strongly infected with the fertility cult that was current in Palestine, with its deification and worship of the forces of nature. The people were abandoning the simpler worship of God to follow this form of nature worship. But Hosea thought of God and the nation as husband and wife, and this adoption of another religion appeared to him an act of conjugal infidelity.

To bring this home to his people he felt it his religious duty to make his own marriage a parable of the nation's sin, and married a notoriously immoral woman, named Gomer, buying her like a slave for a few pieces of silver and a few quarts of barley. In

her unfaithfulness he saw the symbol of Israel's unfaithfulness to God. Israel was no better than an
adulteress, who abandoned an honorable marriage
for base intrigues with faithless lovers.

Gomer's children were given names suggestive of
Israel's disloyalty and disobedience. The boy Jez-
reel[1] recalled Jehu's massacre of Ahab's family in
that city, a crime that was yet to be avenged upon
Jehu's house.[2] The names of the other children,
Lo-ruhamah ("Unpitied") and Lo-ammi ("Not-my-
people")[3] mark them as disowned and repudiated, as
Israel will be disowned and repudiated by God.

This extraordinary story of Hosea's marriage is
told twice: first in the third person, in chapter 1,
and again in the first person, in chapter 3. It is evident from it that the rescue of his nation from its
religious lapse was the one absorbing passion of his
life, compared with which all other ties and hopes—
home and wife and family—were as nothing.

Hosea sometimes includes Judah in his denunciations of Israel, but his appeal is principally addressed to the people of the Northern Kingdom.
The Lord has a quarrel with the inhabitants of the
land, because there is no fidelity, no kindness, and
no knowledge of God in the land:

"Cursing, lying, murder, theft and adultery—
    They break out and one crime follows hard upon
        another."[4]

Their immoral practices are intertwined with their idolatry. Their sons "go apart with harlots and sacrifice with temple-prostitutes."[5] Their daughters, too, are immoral, and their sons' wives are adulterous, but God will not punish them, since their brothers and husbands are no better. This single standard for men and women is a startling thing to find in this ancient oriental prophet.

The indications of Israel's idolatry and its adoption of the fertility cult are numerous in Hosea. Their altars, their sacred pillars, their high places, their Anath and Asherah, their Baals, their idols:

"In Gilgal they sacrifice to demons . . . .
 A maker of images is Ephraim;
 He has set up for himself a fat bull! . . . .
 I loathe your bull, O Samaria! . . . .
 A mechanic made it,
 And it is not God."[6]

For all this betrayal of the love and care of God, the nation must suffer. They sowed the wind, and they shall reap the whirlwind.[7] They shall say to the mountains "Cover us!" and to the hills "Fall upon us!"[8] Because of their wicked deeds God will drive them out of his house.[9] Ephraim shall return to Egypt, and Assyria shall be his king.[10] They shall go to Assyria. Egypt shall gather them, Memphis shall bury them.[11] The calf of Beth Aven shall be carried to Assyria, as tribute to the Great King.[12]

"My God will reject them,
  Because they have not listened to him,
  And they shall become wanderers among the
    nations."[13]

While nothing can avert this penalty of exile, Hosea is not without hope of the ultimate restoration of his people. He is supremely the prophet of the unalterable love of God.

"When Israel was a child, I came to love him,
  And from Egypt I called him. . . . .
  It was I who taught Ephraim to walk,
  I took them up in my arms; . . . .
  How can I give you up, O Ephraim?
  How surrender you, O Israel?"[14]

In the figure of the temporary separation of Hosea and Gomer, the prophet sets forth his expectation of a period of exile, to be followed by the return of Israel to his own land.

"They shall come fluttering like a bird from
    Egypt,
  And like a dove from the land of Assyria,
  And I will bring them back to their homes."
        It is the oracle of the Lord.[15]

"I will betroth you to myself forever;
  I will betroth you to myself in righteousness
    and in justice,
  And in kindness and mercy."[16]

"Whereas it was said to them, 'You are not my
    people,'
It shall be said to them, 'Sons of the living
    God!' "[17]

Hosea's preaching fell a few years later than that
of Amos. Both worked in the days of Jeroboam II,
of Israel, but the work of Amos was over by the
middle of the century, while that of Hosea fell between 745 and 735 B.C. In those years the Assyrian
armies under Tiglath-pileser III were coming nearer
and nearer. In 738, Menahem, king of Israel, sent
tribute to that monarch. In 730, Israel under King
Hoshea became a vassal of Assyria. When he rebelled, about 725, Assyria, now at the zenith of its
power, set out to crush Israel altogether, and in 721
Samaria fell before the Assyrians under Sargon.

Hosea remains the prophet of the unalterable love
of God, as Amos is that of his impartial justice.

SUGGESTIONS FOR STUDY

1. *References:* [1]Hos. 1:4; [2]II Kings, chaps. 9, 10; [3]Hos.
1:6, 9; [4]Hos. 4:2; [5]Hos. 4:14; [6]Hos. 12:11; 4:17; 8:5, 6;
[7]Hos. 8:7; [8]Hos. 10:8; [9]Hos. 9:15; [10]Hos. 11:5; [11]Hos. 9:6;
[12]Hos. 10:5, 6; [13]Hos. 9:17; [14]Hos. 11:1, 3, 8; [15]Hos. 11:11;
[16]Hos. 2:19; [17]Hos. 1:10.

2. How did Hosea's domestic life embody his religious
message?

3. What was the religious condition of Israel in his day?

4. How did the names of Hosea's children bear upon his
work?

5. What penalty does Hosea declare the nation must pay for its sins?

6. When did he prophesy?

7. What was the subsequent fate of Israel?

8. What were the sins he most strongly denounced?

9. Had he any hope for the future of his nation?

10. What is the great religious idea of Hosea?

11. Compare him with Amos.

CHAPTER III

THE BOOK OF MICAH

The crimes and dangers of Israel must have made a very deep impression upon the thoughtful men of the eighth century, for they stirred Micah as well as Amos and Hosea. With him we are brought still nearer to the catastrophe, for he prophesied between 730 and 721 B.C. and in the latter year Samaria fell before the Assyrians under Sargon, and the Northern Kingdom became extinct.

Micah, like Amos, was a peasant. He spoke for the oppressed peasantry, crushed under the tyranny and greed of the rich. His home was the little town of Moresheth Gath, near the Philistine border of Judah. His point of view was rural and provincial rather than urban and metropolitan, and the chief cities of his time seem to him so full of violence and wrong that they are positive crimes:

> What is Jacob's transgression?
> Is it not Samaria?
> And what is Judah's sin?
> Is it not Jerusalem?[1]

These cities seem to the prophet to be built of sin and wrong:

> Who build Zion with blood,
> And Jerusalem with guilt.[2]

Prophets, priests, and judges alike fall under Micah's savage invective:

> Her chiefs pronounce judgment for a bribe,
> And her priests declare oracles for hire,
> And her prophets divine for cash.[3]

> You are my people's foe.
> You rise against those who are at peace.[4]

> For the sake of a mere trifle,
> You take a heavy mortgage.[5]

> They covet fields, and seize them,
> And houses, and carry them off.[6]

> If a man, walking in a false spirit, should lie,
> "I will prophesy to you of wine and strong drink,"
> He would be this people's prophet![7]

> "Is it not your place to know justice,
> You who hate the good and love wickedness,
> Snatching their skin from upon them,
> And their flesh from upon their bones?"[8]

The iron has entered into the soul of Micah, and he champions the cause of his class in no uncertain terms. The ruling classes have betrayed their trust. Israel as well as Judah is guilty, and both alike shall be punished:

> I will turn Samaria into a ruin of the field,
> Into a planted vineyard. . . . .
> All her images shall be burned with fire,

And all her idols I will lay waste.
For from the harlot's hire they were gathered,
And unto the harlot's hire they shall return.[9]

The leaders of Judah still hope that they will
escape. They rely upon the sanctity of the temple,
which they believe God will not permit their enemies to profane:

They lean upon the Lord, saying,
"Is not the Lord in the midst of us?
No misfortune can befall us."[10]

But the punishment that is to fall upon Israel will
involve Judah also:

For her stroke is incurable;
For it has come even to Judah.
It reaches the gate of my people,
Even to Jerusalem.[11]

Therefore, because of you,
Zion shall be plowed like a field,
And Jerusalem shall become a ruin,
And the temple hill a high place in
    a forest.[12]

This bold rustic prophet was in fact the first to
predict the destruction of Jerusalem. It would be
difficult to imagine anything more repugnant and
shocking to Micah's fellow-countrymen. It contra-
dicted their fundamental convictions, both political
and religious, and must have made a profound im-

pression. It was quoted in Jerusalem a hundred
years later, when Jeremiah's predictions of the desolation of the city so infuriated the priests and the
prophets that they called for his execution.[13] Some
of the elders of the land saved him, however, by appealing to the case of Micah, who had said just such
things about Jerusalem and thus caused the people
to repent and reform. For Jerusalem did not fall until 597 B.C., when the Babylonians took it. They destroyed it after their second seizure of it, in 586.

Of the seven chapters of Micah only the first
three can with confidence be called the work of Micah himself. It was probably in about this extent
that the book was known to Jeremiah and his times.
As so often happens, this little collection of dirges in
time gathered to itself kindred poems from later
hands, some of which seemed to supply elements
wanting in Micah's own work.

The second part of our book, chapters 4 and 5,
consists of seven short poems or fragments, none of
them probably earlier than the period of the Exile,
597–538, dealing with the Remnant, the restoration, and the Messianic Age and King. The splendid picture of the Golden Age of peace, 4:1–5, and
of the prince from Bethlehem, 5:1–3, are among the
noblest things in Jewish prophecy:

They will beat their swords into plow-shares,
And their spears into pruning-hooks.

Nation shall not lift up sword against nation,
Nor shall they learn war any more.[14]

And you, O Bethlehem Ephrathah,
Too little to be among the clans of Judah,
From you, one shall come forth for me,
Who shall be ruler over Israel.[15]

That this is really a collection of prophetic poems from different hands is shown by the fact that 4:1-3 is found also in Isa. 2:1-4.

The third part of the book, chapters 6 and 7, is almost equally varied, yet part of these chapters may be as old as the time of Micah, if he lived until the reign of Manasseh. The closing verses, 7:14-20, are clearly as late as the Exile. Denunciations of the city for its sin mingle with visions of the ultimate restoration of Jerusalem. Here is found that perfect description of true religion which is on every account one of the gems of religious literature:

Yet what does the Lord require of you,
But to do justice, and to love kindness,
And to walk humbly with your God?[16]

Small in quantity as what we possess of Micah's own work really is, in fire and vigor he is second to none of the Jewish prophets, but is, as he himself expressed it, full of power

To declare to Jacob his crimes,
And to Israel his sins.[17]

SUGGESTIONS FOR STUDY

1. *References:* [1]Mic. 1:5; [2]Mic. 3:10; [3]Mic. 3:11; [4]Mic. 2:8; [5]Mic. 2:10; [6]Mic. 2:2; [7]Mic. 2:11; [8]Mic. 3:1, 2; [9]Mic. 1:6, 7; [10]Mic. 3:11; [11]Mic. 1:9; [12]Mic. 3:12; [13]Jer. 26:18; [14]Mic. 4:3; [15]Mic. 5:1; [16]Mic. 6:8; [17]Mic. 3:8.

2. When did Micah prophesy?

3. Where did he live?

4. What was his station in life?

5. What great wrongs moved him to preach?

6. What was the burden of his message?

7. What did he think of the cities of Israel and Judah?

8. Why are his prophecies, chaps. 1–3, spoken of as dirges?

9. What did he teach as to the future of Samaria and Jerusalem?

10. How does he compare with Amos and Hosea?

11. What is the character of chaps. 4 and 5?

12. What subjects are dealt with in chaps. 6 and 7?

13. When was Jerusalem captured and when was it destroyed?

CHAPTER IV

THE BOOK OF ISAIAH

In the year 740 B.C., the last year of King Uzziah's life, a young aristocrat of Jerusalem had an extraordinary vision. He beheld God in all his holiness, and was commissioned by him to preach repentance to his obtuse and hard-hearted people, until they should all be swept away to destruction.[1]

It was Isaiah who was called to a task seen to be hopeless from the beginning, which nevertheless must be performed. He was not, like Amos or Micah, a poor peasant from the country. Close as they were to the heart of the people, they beheld the operations of statecraft from afar. But Isaiah was a city man, of high birth, and on familiar terms with the king and the court. His courage, eloquence, and spirit were fully equal to his high station, and have given him a supreme place among the Jewish prophets.

His times were among the most trying in Hebrew history. In 735–734 Syria and Israel made war upon Judah in the effort to force her to join them in resisting Assyria. Every year the Assyrians were coming nearer. They took Damascus in 732, Samaria in 721, and Carchemish in 717. In 715 they defeated Hanno of Gaza in the battle of Raphia. Ashdod was

taken by them in 711, and in 701, under Sennacherib, they invaded Judah itself.

All this Isaiah witnessed, with intense anxiety,
from the vantage-point of the capital of Judah.
Again and again he sought to shape events by ad-
dressing the king with counsels which he felt to be
divinely guided. He was thus a statesman-prophet,
participating actively in the political life of his day,
and interpreting its events in the light of his faith in
God.

Isaiah's prophetic work was done in the reigns of
Uzziah, Jotham, Ahaz, and Hezekiah,[2] but he may
have lived until the times of Manasseh, 693–639
B.C., under whom he is said by tradition to have
suffered martyrdom, by being sawn asunder.

The first twelve chapters of the book consist of
sermons of Isaiah denouncing the sins of Judah—
luxury, injustice, bribery, superstition, idolatry, indulgence, and want of faith—and declaring that
God will destroy the nation because of them. Isaiah's call is described and there is an account of his
interview with Ahaz when Syria and Israel were
threatening Judah. Isaiah foresees the desolation of
the land. He comes to see that the Assyrian is to be
the rod of God's anger and the staff of his fury;[3] he
will sweep through Judah like an overwhelming
flood.[4] A terrible day of judgment is coming, when
the pride of man will be brought low.[5]

Isaiah's children, like Hosea's, were given names

related to his prophecies. One born in the midst of the apprehension of the Syro-Ephraimitic War was given a name to indicate how soon the wealth of Damascus and the spoil of Samaria would be carried away by the king of Assyria.[6] Another was named in honor of the remnant which, Isaiah taught, was all that would return to the service of God.[7] Isaiah's hopelessness as to the mass of the people, reflected in his call,[8] is echoed here, as well as in his purpose to seal up his disregarded testimony, and to seal his teaching in the hearts of the disciples whom he gathered around him,[9] and in whom he saw the beginnings of that remnant which would some day return to the mighty God.[10] Indeed, there is little hope in the preaching of Isaiah. The beautiful prophecies of the Prince of Peace[11] and the Age of Gold[12] reflect the hopes that sprang up long after in the dark years of the Babylonian Exile.

Of the eight parts into which Isaiah may be divided, the second, chapters 13–23, consists of oracles dealing with various crises between the Syro-Ephraimitic War, 735–734 B.C., and the invasion of Sennacherib, 701 B.C. But with these are combined passages like 13:1—14:23 and 21:1–10, which clearly belong to the time of the Exile.

The third part, chapters 24–27, which is probably as late as the time of Alexander the Great, 332 B.C., forms a preface to the fourth part, chapters 28–33, which has mostly to do with the deliverance of Jerusalem; while the fifth part, chapters 34 and 35, forms an eschatological appendix to the preceding section, describing God's judgment upon Edom and the Golden Age to come:

> The wilderness and the parched land shall be
>   glad,
> And the desert shall rejoice and blossom; . . . .
>
> Then shall the eyes of the blind be opened,
> And the ears of the deaf shall be unstopped; . . . .
>
> They shall come to Zion with singing,
> And with everlasting joy upon their heads.[13]

Part VI, chapters 36–39, made up of extracts from II Kings, relates experiences of Isaiah in the time of the invasion by Sennacherib, and forms the conclusion of this main collection of prophecies anciently ascribed to Isaiah, chapters 1–39. Sennacherib's sudden and mysterious raising of the siege of Jerusalem and withdrawal from Judah may have been occasioned by some reverse suffered by his main army which was threatening Egypt.[14] The result was that the doctrine of the inviolability of Jerusalem as the Holy City of God himself became established in Jewish religious thought.[15]

The seventh and eighth parts of the book, chapters 40–55 and 56–66, reflect very different situations and periods from what has gone before. In chapters 40–55 Babylon has replaced Assyria as Judah's overshadowing foe, which has carried the people into exile. The captive nation is the suffering servant of God, and looks to Cyrus, the Persian conqueror, chapter 45, for deliverance from its bondage. Babylon fell before the Persians in 538, and Cyrus began to return the exiles to their homes. These chapters beautifully reflect the joy of the return:

> "Comfort, O comfort my people,"
>   Says your God;
> "Speak to the heart of Jerusalem,
>   And call to her—
>   That her time of service is ended,
>   That her guilt is paid in full." . . . .
>
> On a high mountain get you up,
>   O heralds of good news to Zion!
> Lift up your voice with strength,
>   O heralds of good news to Jerusalem . . . .
> Say to the cities of Judah,
>   "Behold your God!"[16]

The final chapters of the book, Part VIII, chapters 56–66, again present a change of scene. They deal with the situation of the returned exiles, who found it difficult to induce the population of Jerusalem to conform to the legal developments the Hebrew religion had undergone during the Exile, and were probably written about the middle of the fifth century before Christ, not long before the times of Nehemiah and Ezra.

It will be seen that about the great name of Isaiah there has gathered a wide range of prophetic messages, some of them Exilic or post-Exilic; indeed, it is probable that our Book of Isaiah is the combination of several collections of this kind, so that it has become a veritable anthology, or rather a treasury, of the most brilliant and varied Hebrew prophecy.

The work of Isaiah himself is found, with some other material, in the first, second, fourth, and fifth parts of the book, chapters 1–12, 13–23, 28–33, 36–39. His prophecies passed through many editions and sustained many accretions before they reached the form in which they have come down to us, and it cannot have been far from 300 B.C. that the Book of Isaiah received the last of those varied additions that together with the work of Isaiah himself make it the most brilliant and splendid book in all Jewish literature. He was supremely the prophet of the holiness of God.

SUGGESTIONS FOR STUDY

1. *References:* [1]Isa. 6:1–13; [2]Isa. 1:1; [3]Isa. 10:5; [4]Isa. 8:5–8; [5]Isa. 2:17; [6]Isa. 8:4; [7]Isa. 7:3; [8]Isa. 6:9, 10; [9]Isa. 8:16–18; [10]Isa. 10:20, 21; [11]Isa. 9:1–7; [12]Isa. 11:1–9; [13]Isa. 35:1, 5, 10; [14]Isa. 37:36, 37; [15]cf. Isa. 37:35; [16]Isa. 40:1, 2, 9.

2. What part of the Book of Isaiah relates to Isaiah and his work?

3. Where did he live?

4. What was his social station?

5. Describe his call to the prophetic office.

6. What attribute of God most impressed Isaiah?

7. What political events form the background of his work?

8. What hopes of success had Isaiah for his work?

9. What use did he see in it?

10. What measures did he take for its perpetuation?

11. What future for Judah does he foresee?

12. How did other prophecies come to be added to Isaiah's?

13. Who was Cyrus and why was he so glorified by the prophets of the Exile?

14. What parts of the Book of Isaiah deal with the Return?

15. To what period do the closing chapters of the book belong?

CHAPTER V

THE BOOK OF ZEPHANIAH

The prophets felt themselves to be the preachers of a true and lofty religion, which their people for the most part refused and disobeyed. This led them to a mood of deep pessimism. The end, they felt, could be nothing but destruction, utter and hopeless, as Amos had described it, in his fearful vision of the Day of the Lord.[1]

The teaching of the herdsman Amos was echoed more than a century after his time, by a young aristocrat of Jerusalem named Zephaniah, a descendant of King Hezekiah. The Scythians spoken of in Herodotus[2] had made their appearance in Palestine (627 B.C.), and this seemed to Zephaniah to mark the beginning of the end. The destructive Day, of which Amos had spoken, was at last to come, and overwhelm Judah and the sinful nations around.

Later Judaism came to suppose that from an earlier condition of general piety and godliness the Jewish people in the prophets' time had fallen into idolatry and wickedness. It would be truer to think of the prophets in religious development as far in advance of their countrymen, who were still very largely polytheistic and idolatrous. The prophets faced the enormous task of raising these backward masses to something approaching their own moral and religious elevation, and it is not strange that sometimes the undertaking seemed hopeless.

The Scythians had swept into Western Asia from the north, and, encountering the rising power of the Medes, had defeated them, and pressed on into Palestine, with the intention of passing through it to Egypt. But Psammetichus of Egypt met them and made terms with them, so that they presently retired.

Their stay in Palestine was probably not long but it made a deep impression, as both Jeremiah and Zephaniah show. To Zephaniah, these half-savage hordes seemed the prelude to the awful Day of the Lord that the wickedness of the world made him expect. The whole earth must suffer the agonies of judgment:

"I will utterly sweep away everything
From upon the face of the ground.
I will sweep away man and beast;
I will sweep away the fowl of the heavens and the
    fish of the sea.
And I will cause the wicked to stumble,
And I will cut off mankind from upon the face of
    the ground."
It is the oracle of the Lord.[3]

The half-idolatrous people of Judah, with their pagan proclivities, will suffer for their sins:

"And I will stretch out my hand against Judah,
And against all the inhabitants of Jerusalem.
And from this place I will cut off Baal to the last
    remnant,
The name of the priestlings with the priests;
And those who prostrate themselves upon the
    roofs
To the host of the heavens;
And those who prostrate themselves before the
    Lord,
And swear by Milcom;
And those who have withdrawn from following
    the Lord,
And those who have not sought the Lord,
Nor inquired after him."[4]

This terrible prospect of frightful and complete
destruction Zephaniah declares to be close at hand:

Silence before the Lord God,
For the day of the Lord is near at hand! . . . .
Near at hand is the great day of the Lord;
Near and speeding fast!
Near at hand is the bitter day of the Lord.
Then the warrior will cry in terror!
A day of wrath is that day;
A day of trouble and distress,
A day of desolation and waste,
A day of darkness and gloom,
A day of cloud and thundercloud;

A day of trumpet and battle-cry,
Against the fortified cities,
And against the lofty battlements.[5]

The principal damage done by the Scythians in
Palestine seems to have been at the Philistine city
of Ascalon, where, Herodotus says, they destroyed
the temple of Venus (Astarte). Zephaniah has much
to say of Philistia's doom:

Gaza shall be deserted,
And Askelon a waste.
Ashdod—at noon they shall expel her,
And Ekron shall be uprooted. . . . .
The word of the Lord is against you,
O Canaan, land of the Philistines,
And I will destroy you so that there
shall be no inhabitant.[6]

The rising power of the Medes in the farther east
had borne the first brunt of the Scythians' attack,
as their hordes, so like the Mongols in the thirteenth
century, burst into Western Asia. Even Assyria had
been threatened, and the purpose of the invaders
in entering Palestine had been to reach Egypt.
Zephaniah sees in their coming the doom of Assyria
and Egypt:

You, too, O Ethiopians,
Shall be slain by my sword!

And he will stretch out his hand against the
     north,
     And destroy Assyria.
And he will make Nineveh a desolation,
     A drought like the desert.
And herds shall lie down in the midst of her,
     Every beast of the field.
Both screech owl and porcupine
     Shall lodge in her capitals.
The owl shall hoot in the window,
     The bustard on the threshold.
For I will destroy her city.
This is the exultant city,
     That dwelt in security!
That said to itself,
     "I am, and there is none else."
How has she become a ruin,
     A lair for wild beasts.
Everyone that passes by her hisses,
     And shakes his fist![7]

This picture of the desolation of Nineveh recalls
Xenophon's visit to its site more than two hundred
years later, in 401 B.C. He found only "a great wall
lying deserted, belonging to a city called Mespila,
which had once been inhabited by the Medes."[8]

The doom the prophet has foretold for Philistia,
Ethiopia, and Assyria is to overtake Judah also.
Jerusalem is an oppressing city, which has not ac-

cepted correction or drawn near to her God. Idolatry, injustice, and corruption are rampant in Judah:

> Her princes within her are roaring lions;
> Her judges are wolves of the night,
> Who long not for the morning.
> Her prophets are reckless, treacherous men;
> Her priests profane holy things;
> They do violence to the law.[9]

The punishments of the surrounding nations
which should have been a lesson to Judah she has
disregarded. Instead of reforming, her people

> ". . . . have zealously made
> All their doings corrupt."[10]

The announcement of the doom of Moab and
Ammon, 2:8–11, and the closing lyrics of the book,
which deal with the deliverance of Jerusalem and
the future renown of Israel, 3:8–20, are later additions to the work of Zephaniah, and probably belong
to the time of the Exile.

The destruction of Assyria and Judah was not,
however, to be the work of the Scythians, but was
reserved for other hands. Yet it was not long de-
layed. Fifteen years later Assyria fell before the
Medes and Babylonians; Nineveh, the capital, was
captured in 612 B.C., and fifteen years after, in 597,
Jerusalem was taken by the Babylonians. Zephaniah's terrible picture of the Day of the Lord was

revived in the Middle Ages in the great hymn of
Thomas of Celano, A.D. 1250, the first line of which,
"Dies irae, dies illa," is quoted from the Vulgate
Latin translation of Zeph. 1:15: "A day of wrath is
that day!"

SUGGESTIONS FOR STUDY

1. *References:* [1]Amos 5:18–20; 8:7–10; [2]Herodotus, 1.
103–5: "A numerous horde of Scyths, under their king
Madyes, son of Protothyes, burst into Asia in pursuit of the
Cimmerians whom they had driven out of Europe, and
entered the Median territory. . . . . The Scythians, having
invaded Media, were opposed by the Medes, who gave them
battle, but, being defeated, lost their empire. The Scythians
became masters of Asia. After this they marched forward
with the design of invading Egypt. When they reached Palestine, however, Psammetichus the Egyptian king met them
with gifts and prayers, and prevailed on them to advance no
farther. On their return, passing through Ascalon, a city of
Syria, the greater part of them went their way without doing
any damage; but some few who lagged behind pillaged the
temple of Celestial Venus. . . . . The dominion of the Scythians over Asia lasted eight and twenty years, during which
time their insolence and oppression spread ruin on every
side. . . . . They scoured the country and plundered every
one of whatever they could" (Rawlinson's translation);
[3]Zeph. 1:2, 3; [4]Zeph. 1:4–6; [5]Zeph. 1:7, 14–16; [6]Zeph. 2:4, 5;
[7]Zeph. 2:12–15; [8]Anabasis, iii:4. 10; [9]Zeph. 3:3, 4; [10]Zeph.
3:7.

2. What menacing situation led Zephaniah to prophesy?

3. From what earlier prophet did he take his text?

4. What is the subject of his prophecy?

5. What fate does he anticipate for the nations around
Judah?

6. What is Judah herself going to experience?

7. What does Zephaniah think of Judah and Jerusalem?

8. What does he describe as their chief failings?

9. When did Nineveh fall?

10. What remains of Nineveh did Xenophon find when he passed that way with the Ten Thousand two centuries later?

11. What do you think of Zephaniah's moral ideals?

12. What do you think of his literary skill?

CHAPTER VI

THE BOOK OF NAHUM

The Jew has always had a strong race-consciousness, a keen sense of his Jewish blood and heritage. The most conspicuous example of this attitude among the prophets is Nahum, who is also probably the greatest poet among them.

Nahum is stirred to write by the impending fall of Nineveh, which seems to be immediately in prospect, if it has not just actually taken place. Nineveh had long overshadowed and threatened the little kingdom of Judah, but now that cruel, devastating empire is facing its own doom. Half a century before, about 661 B.C., the Assyrians under Ashurbanipal had captured and plundered Thebes, the ancient capital of Egypt, but now their time has come and their own capital is to be taken and sacked. This allusion to the fall of Thebes helps us to date the prophecy of Nahum. He evidently writes after that event, and when the fall of Nineveh before the Babylonians and Medes is a certainty of the near future. Nineveh fell in 612 B.C. and Nahum probably uttered this prophecy about that time.

The Assyrians had for centuries been the terror of the smaller kingdoms of Western Asia. One by one

they had fallen before her, Israel among the rest.
Once Sennacherib had invaded Judah itself and laid
siege to Jerusalem. This event of ninety years before is probably what is referred to in 1:11:

> Did not one go forth from you plotting evil
>   against the Lord,
> Counselling rascality?

For the Assyrians were not, like some conquerors,
benefactors of the peoples they conquered. And
while the nations of the ancient East were all cruel,
the Assyrians, if not actually the most cruel of them
all, certainly took the most satisfaction in recording
their atrocities in their inscriptions.

All this and much more besides lies back of the
prophecy of Nahum. If we could assemble in our
minds all that we nowadays most hate and abhor in
the modern world, it would be pale and insignificant
compared with the mass of memories and pictures
that filled the mind of Nahum as he thought of
Nineveh and the doings of the Assyrians through
three centuries of invasion, deportation, and bar-
barity. Only thus can we fairly understand the bitterness of his hatred. And in the destruction of
Assyria he sees God's punishment of her for her
crimes.

The Assyrians had built up by sheer force of arms
the greatest empire the world had yet seen. They
had developed the provincial system of organiza-

tion, and to keep their conquests in subjection had devised the policy of deporting conquered peoples to other distant parts of their empire, where they would be less likely to rebel. Thus Sargon had carried more than twenty-seven thousand people away from Samaria, in 721, and the long grief of exile was added to the humiliation of defeat. Judah and Jerusalem had narrowly escaped a similar fate twenty years later.

But now a power had arisen in the East that could actually try conclusions with Assyria herself and push her from her place. Centuries before, the Babylonians had been the masters of the Eastern world, and now after a long period of quiescence, under a new dynasty they resumed their old position. They were enabled to do this by the appearance of the Medes in the farther east, and their combined forces enabled them to capture Nineveh, conquer the Assyrian Empire, and divide it between them.

Nahum's eyes are fixed upon the dramatic point in this great upheaval—the capture of Nineveh. He greets her downfall with unrestrained delight. The confusion of the siege and sack of the city give his unequaled descriptive powers ample scope:

Oh city, bloody throughout,
Full of lies and booty!
Prey ceases not.

> The crack of the whip, and the noise of the rum-
>   bling wheel,
> And the galloping horse, and the jolting chariot,
> The charging horseman, and the flashing sword,
> And the glittering spear, and a multitude of slain,
> And a mass of bodies, and no end to the corpses!
> They stumble over the corpses!¹

The earlier prophets had been greatly impressed
with the military organization of Assyria. Isaiah described it in one of his most brilliant passages:

> No loin-girdle of his is loosed,
> No sandal-thong is snapped;
> His arrows are sharpened,
> His bows are all bent;
> His horses' hoofs are counted like flint,
> His wheels like the whirlwind.²

Nahum exultingly describes it as now driven to
self-defense:

> The shatterer is come up against you;
> Keep the rampart;
> Watch the road; brace your loins.
> Strengthen your forces to the utmost. . . . .

> The chariots will rage in the streets,
> Dashing to and fro in the open spaces.
> Their appearance will be like that of torches,
> Darting about like lightning.
> He summons his nobles; they stumble as they
>   go;

They hasten to the wall,
And the battering ram is set up.

The gates of the rivers are opened
And the palace melts away.
Its mistress is brought forth; she goes into
    captivity,
While her maidens mourn,
Moaning like the sound of doves,
Beating upon their breasts.
And Nineveh is like a pool of water,
Whose water escapes.

There is emptiness, and desolation, and
    waste,
And a melting heart and trembling knees;
And anguish is in all loins,
And the faces of all of them become livid.
Where is the den of the lions,
And the cave of the young lions,
Whither the lion went bringing in spoil,
The lion's cub, with none to disturb?[3]

Nineveh is now to suffer what she had so often
made others suffer. Half a century before she had
destroyed Thebes:

"Are you any better than Thebes,
    That sat by the great Nile,
    (Water was around her)
    Whose rampart was the sea,

Whose wall was water? . . . .
Yet even she became an exile;
She went into captivity. . . . .
You too shall reel and swoon,
You too shall seek refuge from the foe. . . . .

"Draw yourself waters for the siege;
        strengthen your forts. . . . .
But there fire shall devour you,
The sword shall cut you off.

"Your shepherds slumber, O king of Assyria,
    ' Your nobles sleep! . . . .
There is no healing for your wound,
    Your hurt is incurable.
Everyone who shall hear the news about you
    Will clap his hands over you.
For against whom has your malice not con-
    tinually gone forth?"[4]

To Nahum's fiery oracles a later hand has pre-
fixed an acrostic poem on the avenging Wrath of
God, 1:2–10, probably in the time of the Exile,
when such alphabetic poems began to become common. It has the effect of making Nahum's song of
triumph over Nineveh an illustration of God's deal-
ings with the wicked.

SUGGESTIONS FOR STUDY

1. *References:* [1]Nah. 3:1–3; [2]Isa. 5:27, 28; [3]Nah. 2:1,
4–8, 10, 11; [4]Nah. 3:8, 10, 11, 14, 15, 18, 19.

2. What political situation led Nahum to utter his
prophecy?

3. What was the substance of his message?

4. What had Assyria done to stir him so deeply?

5. What combination of forces led to the fall of Nineveh?

6. What use does Nahum make of the fate of Thebes?

7. What was the policy of the Assyrians in dealing with conquered peoples?

8. What scenes does Nahum most realistically describe?

9. What do you think of his poetry?

10. What relation does 1:1–10 bear to the rest of the book?

11. Does Nahum take up the question of forgiving one's enemies?

CHAPTER VII

THE BOOK OF DEUTERONOMY

It was the eighteenth year of the reign of Josiah. The half-heathen reigns of Manasseh and Amon were over, and under King Josiah efforts were being made to undo the evil effects of their times. Among other reforms the temple was repaired, and in the course of this work somewhere in its recesses an old book of law was discovered. A dramatic account of the incident is found in II Kings, chapters 22 and 23. The book was taken to the young king and read to him, and it led him to further reforms in the religious life of the nation. He put a stop to the idolatrous practices of the people, sought to confine sacrifice to the temple in Jerusalem alone, and had the Passover celebrated in Jerusalem by all the people.

Just these things are prescribed in the Book of Deuteronomy, and it was that book, in substance, that was found and put into effect by Josiah in 621 B.C.

Deuteronomy is the embodiment of the long struggle of the prophets with the old idolatry of the land and with the foreign forms of worship that kept creeping in. In it the great prophetic ideals of religion, as something that should pervade and purify the whole life of the nation, are powerfully presented. The reforms undertaken by Hezekiah (721–693)[1] had been more than undone under Manasseh (693–639),[2] but now Josiah made the most vigorous attempt in the whole history of the kingdom to carry out the prophetic ideals. Isaiah had taught that the Temple in Jerusalem was the dwelling-place of God, but now it was conceived to be the only sanctuary where he could be acceptably worshiped.

The prophets had always emphasized morals rather than ritual, and had laid little stress upon sacrifice as a way of pleasing God. But now they laid hold of it as a concession to the practical religious needs of the people, purifying and interpreting it, so as to make it a real religious symbol of obedience and devotion to God. Prophetic and priestly interests thus combine in what we know as Deuteronomy. The ceremonial worship of God was to carry with it high ideals of personal morality and social justice.

These ideals were embodied in a series of laws, which were felt to represent the aims and purposes of Moses himself, their great liberator, to whom they looked back as the founder of their religion, six hundred years before. These laws are an expansion and revision of an earlier code which had long existed, and which is preserved in Exod. 20:20— 23:33, the so-called "Book of the Covenant." Some things contained in that code were entirely out of date when Deuteronomy was written, like the command to exterminate the Canaanites; but in general Deuteronomy reformulates and reinterprets existing laws, seeking to adjust them to contemporary conditions and fill them with a nobler spirit and with loftier sanctions. Obedience is to rise not from fear or self-interest but from the people's love of God:

"Listen, O Israel; the Lord is our God, the Lord alone; so you must love the Lord your God with all your mind and all your heart and all your strength."[3]

How had the mysterious book of law which Hilkiah found come into existence? It was probably written in the dark days of Manasseh, when the prophets who had guided the reformation under Hezekiah had been put to death or silenced. Isaiah is supposed to have suffered martyrdom at that time and Micah too may have perished. Heathenism once more pervaded the land. The prophets could not speak; their fair hopes for a righteous and God-fearing nation were cruelly disappointed. Some survivor of their group, however, solaced himself in secret, about 675–650 B.C., by rewriting the old law in the new prophetic spirit, and casting it into a great prophetic appeal, in the form of an oration by Moses himself. And years after, when Manasseh was dead, this masterpiece of prophetic religion came to light and became the first Bible of the Jewish people. In it, rather than in the prophets, we have the actual nucleus of the Jewish scriptures. From this time on Judaism rallies about a book, and that book is Deuteronomy.

The unknown prophet who wrote Deuteronomy was one of the chief masters of Hebrew prose. He put his work in the form of an oration addressed by Moses to the Israelites as the people approached the promised land, toward the end of the forty years' wandering, when Moses was about to leave them. It is his great valedictory.

It comprises Deuteronomy, chapters 5–26 and 28, and seeks to revise and refine the old law in the spirit of the prophets. Chapters 5–11 form the introduction and chapter 28 the conclusion. The main legal section, chapters 12–26, represents a reorganization of current laws, including the Book of the Covenant, Exod. 20:20—23:33, on a higher plane, with more regard to social and human values. There is more justice, and more recognition and protection for women, slaves, employes, aliens, and the poor.

The Book of the Covenant was itself the fruit of a long development, and reflects a much more primitive time than that of Deuteronomy. It may date from the reform under Asa, king of Judah, about 900 B.C.[4] It in turn grew out of the still more primitive law-code of Exodus, chapter 34—the Little Book of the Covenant, which is probably the germ of the whole Hebrew legislation.

The religious laws of Deuteronomy are particularly interesting. The old local sanctuaries are to be done away; only in Jerusalem can sacrifices be offered to God. The multiplicity of places of sacrifice had made return to idolatry too easy, and against every form of idolatry and paganism Deuteronomy is very severe. The Passover, too, must be celebrated in Jerusalem and nowhere else. This unification of religion in Jerusalem made its control in the interests of monotheism much easier and more effective.[5]

The reforms of Judaism contemplated in Deuteronomy had definite and significant results; Josiah did his utmost to carry them out. But even greater was the influence of the Book of Deuteronomy itself upon contemporary and subsequent Jewish writers. The ideas it embodied powerfully and usefully affected later religious thought, and its appearance marked a new epoch in Jewish religion. It is especially significant as an effort to blend priestly with prophetic ideals of religion, and to fill the sacrificial forms of worship with spiritual meaning.

To this masterpiece of the prophetic spirit were later added chapters 1–4, 27, and 29–34, probably when about 350 B.C. it was wrought into the great encyclopedia of Jewish history, religion, and law which we know as the Hexateuch. Its Greek name, Deuteronomy, the "Second Giving of the Law," was applied to it when in the third century before Christ it was translated, along with Genesis, Exodus, Leviticus, and Numbers, into Greek. And beyond any other single book in the Old Testament it is the germ of what we know as the Bible.

1. *References:* [1]II Kings 18:4, 5; [2]II Kings 21:3–16; [3]Deut. 6:4, 5; [4]I Kings 15:9–15; [5]Deut. 16:5, 6, 11, 15, 16.

2. Read Deut., chaps. 5–11, which has been said to embody the noblest religious and social thought ever expressed.

3. Compare Deut., chaps. 12–26, with Exod. 20:20—23:33, the "Book of the Covenant."

4. Compare Exod. 20:20—23:33 with Exod., chap. 34, the "Little Book of the Covenant." Which seems to be derived from the other?

5. When was the Book of Deuteronomy written?

6. When was it adopted as law?

7. What did its writer intend to accomplish by it?

8. What are its leading religious ideas?

9. What reforms in worship was it meant to effect?

10. In what literary form is it cast?

11. What were some of its results?

12. What priestly interests did it serve?

13. What prophetic ideals did it embody?

CHAPTER VIII

THE BOOK OF HABAKKUK

The Hebrew prophets believed firmly in a righteous God, but they saw the world falling a prey to one cruel and brutal tyranny after another, with no apparent reference to right or wrong. Judah herself was wicked enough; her sins roused the prophet Habakkuk to cry to God for punishment upon her. He uttered his prophecies in the last years of the Kingdom of Judah, in the reign of Jehoiakim, 608–597 B.C., a few years after the fall of Assyria before the Medes and Babylonians. The prophets rejoiced in the downfall of Assyria, but it soon became evident that in the Babylonians a new power just as ruthless had taken its place.

Habakkuk is distressed at the violence, injustice, and wrongdoing that prevail in Judah:

> How long, O Lord, must I cry for help,
>   And thou not hear?
> And call out to thee "Violence,"
>   And thou not save?[1]

The solution of the matter presently comes to him. The Babylonians are to be God's instrument of punishment. They will come down upon Judah and destroy it. This must have been in the days of

Babylonia's rise to power, after the fall of Assyria and before the fall of Jerusalem. God answers the prophet's appeal:

"Look out upon the nations and see,
　And be utterly amazed.
　For a deed is being done in your days
　That you would not believe, were it told you.
　For behold I am raising up the Chaldeans,
　That savage and impetuous nation,
　That marches through the breadth of the earth,
　To seize habitations that are not his own.

"Terrible and dreadful is he; . . . .
　Swifter than leopards are his horses,
　And keener than wolves of the desert. . . . .
　Terror marches before him;
　And he gathers up captives like sand.
　He makes scorn of kings;
　And rulers are a joke to him!
　He laughs at all fortresses,
　And heaps up dirt and captures them."[2]

The fall of Nineveh in 612 B.C. before the Babylonians and Medes must have astonished the ancient world, so long accustomed to Assyrian supremacy. And now this new power is turning westward, toward Palestine, and it begins to look as though Judah's time had come and the sins the prophet had denounced were to be punished. The Babylonians had met the Egyptians at Carchemish

in 605 B.C. and decisively defeated them, driving
them out of Palestine, which they had long controlled, and leaving Judah at the mercy of the vic-
tors. In so short a time had the new power of Babylon overcome both the great powers of the day—
Assyria and Egypt. It was indeed an incredible
achievement, "a deed that you would not believe
were it told you."

The dialogue continues. The prophet sees that
the sinfulness of Judah is to be punished, but only
by a power more sinful still, the cruel and brutal
Babylonians. Must this series of violent oppressors
go on forever? Will God keep silent when the wicked swallows up him that is more righteous than
himself? To the conqueror men are no more than so
many fish that he gathers in his net:

> Shall he keep on emptying his net forever,
> And never cease slaying the nations?[3]

Like a watchman upon his lookout the prophet
looks expectantly to God for light upon this question:

> I will take my stand upon my watch-tower,
> And station myself upon the rampart;
> And watch to see what he will say to me,
> And what answer he will make to my complaint.[4]

The answer comes to him:

> "Write the vision clearly upon the tablets,
> That one may read it on the run. . . . .

Verily, the wicked man—I take no pleasure in
 him;
But the righteous lives by reason of his faithful-
 ness.
How much less shall the faithless man live, ...
Shall not all these take up a taunt song against
 him,
And a sharp satire against him, saying,
'Woe to him who enriches himself with what is not
 his own'? . . . .
You will become spoil for them!
Because you have spoiled many nations,
All the rest of the peoples shall spoil you."[5]

God takes no pleasure in the triumphs of the
wicked, but the upright shall live because of his
faithfulness; that is, his devotion will be in some
sense rewarded. Habakkuk has raised the problem
of evil, and the solution he offers for it seems no
better than the old, timeworn Hebrew solution that
piety will bring prosperity. Yet later minds found
in it a deeper meaning, and long after it became a
war-cry for Paul and Luther.

To God's woe pronounced against the rapacious
invaders the prophet adds four more, for their ag-
gression, violence, and idolatry.[6] We seem now to
be in the times of the invasion and conquest of Judah, the fall of Jerusalem, and the carrying of the
Jews into captivity, 597 B.C. The Babylonian who

had at first appeared as the instrument of God's wrath is now seen to be the archenemy of his people, cruel and hateful. Plunder, bloodshed, violence, and wrong are everywhere. But the tyrant's time will come, and he in his turn will go down to destruction before some new invader. The heathen nations do indeed wear themselves out for naught:

> But the earth shall be filled with the knowledge of
>   the glory of the Lord,
> As the waters cover the sea![7]

To be conquered and humiliated by idolaters was particularly distressing to the prophets. It seemed as though their religion had suffered defeat, for to the oriental mind a nation's gods stood or fell with the nation. But it came to be clear to the prophets that the deepest things in their faith were not at the mercy of Assyrian, Egyptian, or Babylonian armies, and that the triumph of the idols was not real:

> Woe to him who says to wood, "Wake up,"
> To a dumb stone, "Arise."
> Can it give oracles? . . . .
> But the Lord is in his holy temple;
> Be silent before him, all the earth![8]

Yet this reference to the temple as standing seems to put this woe against idolatry into a later time than the fall of Jerusalem before Nebuchadnezzar in 597, and the destruction of the Temple by the Babylonians in 586, and it probably belongs, like the following chapter, to the period of the rebuilt Temple, after the Exile.

The last chapter of the Book of Habakkuk is a psalm, written long after, probably even after the Exile, for it contains many reminiscences of Hebrew literature, especially Ps. 77:17–20. It describes God in stormy majesty as the judge of the nations, and in one of the noblest pieces of Hebrew poetry expresses that indomitable trust in God—whatever happens—which had been the underlying conviction of Habakkuk:

> Though the fig tree do not flourish,
> And there be no fruit on the vines;
> Though the product of the olive fail,
> And the fields yield no food;
> Though the flock be cut off from the fold,
> And there be no cattle in the stalls;
> Yet I will exult in the Lord;
> I will rejoice in my victorious God!
> God, the Lord, is my strength;
> And he makes my feet like the feet of hinds,
> And makes me walk upon my heights.[9]

SUGGESTIONS FOR STUDY

1. *References:* [1]Hab. 1:2; [2]Hab. 1:5–10; [3]Hab. 1:17; [4]Hab. 2:1; [5]Hab. 2:2, 4–8; [6]Hab. 2:9–20; [7]Hab. 2:14; [8]Hab. 2:19, 20; [9]Hab. 3:17–19.

2. With Hab. 2:14 compare Isa. 11:9. Which seems to you a quotation of the other?

3. With Hab. 3:3 compare Deut. 33:2. Which seems to you to have been influenced by the other?

4. With Hab. 3:10–12, 15 compare Ps. 77:17–20. Which seems to you a quotation of the other?

5. With Hab. 3:18 compare Mic. 7:7. Which seems to you to have quoted the other?

6. With Hab. 3:19 compare II Sam. 22:33, 34 and Ps. 18:34. Is there literary dependence here?

7. What aroused Habakkuk to prophesy?

8. What view did he come to take of the rise of Babylon?

9. What did he think would be her fate?

10. What great problem did Habakkuk raise? Did he solve it?

11. What is the message of the psalm that now concludes the book?

CHAPTER IX

THE BOOK OF JEREMIAH

The Scythian hordes whose appearance in Palestine had seemed to Zephaniah to herald the dreadful Day of the Lord awoke the spirit of prophecy in another young Jew, named Jeremiah. He lived in the village of Anathoth, four miles northeast of Jerusalem. But his sermons, unlike Zephaniah's, are not confined to the time of the Scythian invasion but reflect the history of his people through a period of forty years, 627–586 B.C. These years witnessed great changes in the empires of the East and in the fortunes of Judah: the Scythian advance (627), the fall of Assyria (612), the death of Josiah at Megiddo (609), the rise of Babylon, her defeat of Egypt at Carchemish (605) and consequent control of Judah, the capture of Jerusalem and first deportation (597), and the destruction of the city and final deportation (586). And early in this period occurred the religious reforms of Josiah and the introduction of the Deuteronomic law, discovered in 621. Through these momentous years the great voice of Jeremiah makes itself heard now and again, in crises of political or religious life.

Jeremiah felt himself called to be a prophet to the nations, with authority

> To root up and to pull down, to wreck and to
> ruin, to build and to plant.[1]

Like a boiling pot out of the north all the kingdoms of the earth seemed to come against Judah; as Israel, Syria, and Assyria had in the years before come down against her, now the Scythians were coming, and later the Babylonians were to come.[2] In all this Jeremiah sees the just punishment of his people's idolatry and wickedness.

Jeremiah felt quite unequal to the task set for him:

> "Ah, Lord God! I cannot speak;
> For I am only a boy."
> But the Lord said to me,
> "Do not say, 'I am only a boy';
> For to all to whom I send you shall you go,
> And all that I command you shall you speak."[3]

Jeremiah was by nature a shrinking, sensitive man, but he developed a heroic tenacity in his difficult and thankless work. He did not hesitate to denounce the priests and prophets as well as the kings and princes of Judah for their shortcomings: "On your hands is found the blood of the innocent poor."[4]

It is not only the character of Jeremiah that is appealing and affecting; his literary art is equally striking and has enriched the diction of the world.

The sermons of chapters 1–6 belong to the years 627–621 B.C., before the Deuteronomic reformation.

The changes demanded by Deuteronomy must have been welcome to Jeremiah, as far as their discouragement of idolatry was concerned, but the emphasis they laid upon the Temple, sacrifice, and the formal exercises of religion was extremely distasteful to him, for he put the emphasis in religion upon moral uprightness and the inner life (chaps. 7, 8, 11).

The sin and failure of his people stir Jeremiah to the bitterest outcries; no wonder he has been called the "Weeping Prophet":

> Is there no balm in Gilead?
> Is there no physician there? . . . .
> Oh that my head were waters,
> And mine eyes a fountain of tears,
> That I might weep day and night
> For the slain of the daughter of my people!
> Oh that I had in the desert
>   A traveller's inn,
> That I might leave my people,
>   and be quit of them.
> For they are all adulterers,
>   a company of traitors. . . . .
> They cheat each one his neighbor,
> And no one speaks the truth.[5]

It is in kindness, justice, and uprightness that God delights, and he will punish the nation with destruction:

"I will make Jerusalem a heap of ruins,
        a lair of jackals."[6]

After the death of King Josiah in 609, Jeremiah
caused his sermons and memoirs to be written down,
and a roll containing them was laid before King
Jehoiakim, in the fourth year of his reign, 604 B.C.[7]
The king scornfully cut the roll to pieces with his
knife and burned it up. This led Jeremiah to have a
second, more comprehensive collection made by his
secretary Baruch, and this, together with biographi-
cal material by his disciples, formed the basis of our
Book of Jeremiah, which may be described as at
least the third edition of Jeremiah. The first edition, sent to Jehoiakim, probably contained little
more than chapters 1–17.

The final overthrow of Judah came at the end of a
long series of disasters. Josiah had been killed at
Megiddo (609) by Necho of Egypt, who thus became master of Judah. But Necho was defeated at
Carchemish in 605 by the Babylonian crown-prince
Nebuchadnezzar, and so Judah became a vassal of
Babylon. But the Jewish king Jehoiakim withheld
his tribute, and Nebuchadnezzar in 597 besieged
and captured Jerusalem and carried into captivity
ten thousand men of the better class. Zedekiah, the
puppet king he appointed, being encouraged by
Egypt, rebelled, and in 586 the city was again taken,
a great body of captives was transported to Baby-

lonia, and the Temple, the pride of all Jewish hearts, was destroyed.

Most of these tragic happenings are reflected in the pages of Jeremiah. He had been the friend of Josiah, and the unsparing critic of Jehoiakim. Zedekiah consulted him but would not take his advice to offer no resistance to the Babylonian army.[8] Jeremiah's bold prediction of the destruction of Jerusalem and the Temple had offended the religious and political feelings of both court and priesthood and involved him in the gravest danger.[9] For a hundred years the inviolability of the Temple had been a cherished Jewish conviction. Jeremiah was imprisoned and put in the stocks. He was lowered into a cistern and left to die, but the intercession of an Ethiopian eunuch saved his life.[10] When the city was taken for the second time and the Temple was destroyed,[11] he found himself left behind in a desolated and hopeless Judah, from which the glory had utterly departed.[12] Even then his troubles were not over. The turbulent remnant rose against their new rulers and killed them, and to escape the consequences, most of the Jewish community fled to Egypt for safety, taking Jeremiah with them.[13] There he disappears from our view, still protesting against idolatry and striving to keep his miserable companions faithful to their religion.[14]

No Hebrew prophet reveals himself to us so completely as Jeremiah. His anguish over his hopeless task, his resentment against God himself for his situation, his extreme sensitiveness of spirit, combined with his courage and tenacity of purpose, make him a unique figure, at once pathetic and heroic. It was his hard task to distinguish Jewish religion from Jewish national fortunes, and show that they did not stand or fall together; that the Jewish faith did not perish with the Temple, and above all that religion is an individual and inner, not a national and outward, possession and experience.[15] This perception is the great contribution of Jeremiah to Israel's religion.

SUGGESTIONS FOR STUDY

1. *References:* [1]Jer. 1:10; [2]Jer. 1:13–16; [3]Jer. 1:6, 7; [4]Jer. 2:34 (cf. 5:31); [5]Jer. 8:22; 9:1, 2, 5; [6]Jer. 9:11; [7]Jer., chap. 36; [8]Jer. 38:14–28; [9]Jer., chap. 26; [10]Jer. 37:11—38:13; [11]Jer. 39:1, 2, 4–10; [12]Jer. 39:14; [13]Jer. 41:1–3; 43:4–6; [14]Jer., chap. 44; [15]Jer. 31:27–34.

2. In what period of Jewish history did Jeremiah live?

3. Name some important events of that period.

4. Where was his early home?

5. What great movement is reflected in his early preaching?

6. Read Jer. 4:5—6:26 in the light of that movement.

7. What other prophet dealt with it?

8. What steps did Jeremiah take for the preservation of his memoirs and sermons? Read chap. 36.

9. What was his attitude to the Deuteronomic reformation of Josiah? Read chaps. 7, 8, 11.

10. What was his relation to Josiah? To Jehoiakim? To Zedekiah?

11. What prophecies of Jeremiah made him unpopular with the court and the priesthood?

12. What was the character of Jeremiah?

13. What were the leading traits in his message?

14. What is the story of Jeremiah's Temple address and what came of it? Read chap. 26.

15. In connection with the defeat of the Egyptians at Carchemish read chap. 46.

16. For Jeremiah's inner life read Jer. 15:10–21; 20:7–18.

17. For his characteristic message read Jer. 31:27–34.

CHAPTER X

THE BOOK OF EZEKIEL

The most creative period in Hebrew literature was the Exile. It was only when it was uprooted from its own land and social habits that the Hebrew genius fully expressed itself and the Hebrew faith rose to its true stature.

The first of the exiles to lift up his voice was Ezekiel. He was a priest who had been carried into captivity in the first deportation of 597 B.C., when the better class of the population of Jerusalem was taken. Ezekiel dates his visions from that sad event,[1] which is also described as the exile of King Jehoiachin.[2] Jehoiachin was the unfortunate son of Jehoiakim who became king at eighteen and after a reign of three months was taken captive by Nebuchadnezzar and carried to Babylon, where he remained in prison until the death of his conqueror, thirty-seven years later. Nebuchadnezzar's successor, Evil-merodach, released him, and for the rest of his life he was treated with consideration.[3] Even in his exile and captivity Ezekiel evidently regarded him as the rightful king of Judah, as did the authors of the closing paragraph of Jeremiah and of II Kings.

Ezekiel was called to prophesy in the fifth year of

Jehoiachin's exile, 592 B.C. Ezekiel was then living with other exiles at Tel Abib, on the banks of the Chebar, the Grand Canal in Babylonia. Much of his prophecy is cast in the form of visions. His first vision was of four living creatures drawing a topaz chariot supporting a sapphire throne, with the shining figure of God, who commissioned him to speak in his name to the rebellious household of Israel. His task is to be as hopeless as Isaiah's was:

"They will not listen to you, for they will not listen to me. . . . . But I will make you as hardfaced and stubborn as they; I will make you like adamant, harder than flint."[4]

Ezekiel's call laid on him a great responsibility. He was appointed watchman to the household of Israel. If he failed to warn them, their blood would be upon his head. The prophet felt a terrible responsibility for the moral life of his people, now in their exile in the midst of a triumphant idolatry more likely than ever to wander from their faith.

From distant Babylonia, Ezekiel watched the progress of events at home in Judah. He felt the unrepentant wickedness of the Bloody City.[5] He foresaw the final destruction of city and Temple. He saw the Glory of the Lord depart in awful splendor from the Temple.[6] In this vision, as in the account of his call (chap. 1), his symbolism is colored by what he had seen of Babylonian art, with its

giant winged bulls, or cherubs, with human faces.
Ezekiel shows the influence of earlier Jewish prophets too—Hosea, Isaiah, Jeremiah—but he is no
mere imitator, but a creative and original mind.

His writings are full of vision, allegory, and symbol. His great vision of the Glory of God is thought
of as pre-eminently the Vision of Ezekiel,[7] but hardly less significant is the Vision of the Valley of the
Dry Bones,[8] in which he foretells the return of the
exiles to Judah. Of his allegories, those of the Faithless Wife,[9] the Eagles and the Vine,[10] and the Two
Sisters, Samaria and Jerusalem,[11] are the most im-
pressive. And by striking symbolic actions he pic-
tured and interpreted the second fall of Jerusalem
of 586 B.C., and the second deportation.[12] His re-
fusal to mourn over the death of his wife was also a
symbolic prophecy.[13]

Ezekiel gives a dramatic account of the arrival of
a messenger with the news that what he had so long
foretold had happened; Jerusalem had again fallen.[14]
This confirmation of his earlier unwelcome preaching must have greatly strengthened his position as a
prophet, yet the people were too much absorbed in
their business pursuits to give much heed to him:

"You are to them like a singer of love-songs, with
a beautiful voice, and able to play well on the instrument: they listen to your words, but they will
not obey them. Only when the hour comes—and it

is coming—they shall know that a prophet has been in the midst of them."[15]

Ezekiel is the great representative of the religious worth of the individual and of personal responsibility in religion. Jeremiah had declared religion to be an individual matter, and Ezekiel carries that teaching out to important conclusions.[16] The exiled Jews were inclined to think they were paying for their fathers' sins. But Ezekiel declares that iniquity and uprightness are not hereditary; they are the fruit of the individual's own choices. No man, no matter how good he is, can save another.[17] Even within the life of the individual, if an upright man does wrong, he will be held accountable for it, and if an unrighteous man repents and reforms, he will live and not die.

"Repent, then, ... get you a new heart and a new spirit. Why should you die, O household of Israel? For I have no pleasure in the death of anyone who dies," is the oracle of the Lord God.[18]

Ezekiel declares almost everything he says to be the oracle of God, going farther in this than any of his prophetic predecessors. Most of his prophecies that can be dated were uttered between 592 and 584 B.C., but they were probably committed to writing about 570 B.C. or soon after. They are not arranged in chronological order, but the dates Ezekiel connects with them cover a period of about twenty-five years, from 592 to 567 B.C.

In general, chapters 1–24 gather up the prophecies of judgment uttered before the final destruction of Jerusalem in 586 B.C. Chapters 25–32 pronounce judgment upon the nations surrounding Judah, and probably belong to the time after the complete collapse of Judah, when these heathen peoples seemed to have triumphed over her and to be glorying in her downfall. Chapters 33–48 look forward to the restoration of the nation and the national worship.

Ezekiel foresaw a gigantic attack, a kind of grand offensive against the future nation, when the heathen powers of the world should unite under the leadership of Gog of the land of Magog, to destroy God's people Israel, so happily settled again in Palestine, at the center of the earth.[19] But when that happened, God himself, with all the forces of nature, would rise in their defense and destroy the impious Gog and all his host.

Ezekiel explained the destruction of the Temple by the fact that God had abandoned it. This is the meaning of his vision of the Departure of the Glory of God from it.[20] After the second capture of the city and the demolishing of the Temple, his thoughts turned to a future day when the purified exiles should be brought back to their land and when the Glory should return to the Temple hill. The old sanctuary had been profaned by the admission to it of idola-

trous worship; it was such things that had driven
God's presence from it. But Ezekiel now looked
forward to a new sanctuary, carefully guarded and
walled about, and protected from any possible prof-
anation, with an inner court for the priests and an
outer court for the people. The service was to be in
the hands of the old Jerusalem priesthood, the sons
of Zadok, while the menial duties should be performed by the Levites, who had been the priests of
the old local sanctuaries. The cultus itself was also
to be reformed and new sin-offerings instituted to
insure the holiness of the people. To such a temple
God would return.

This new law of the Temple is developed in chapters 40–46, and reminds us that Ezekiel is not only a
prophet but a priest, who looked forward to the
restoration of the worship of God in the Temple on
a nobler plane and on behalf of a reformed people.
Prophet though he was, as a priest he sought to
mold the religious life of his people into stricter
ecclesiastical terms. For this reason he has been
called the Father of Judaism.

SUGGESTIONS FOR STUDY

1. *References:* [1]Ezek. 33:21; [2]Ezek. 1:2; [3]II Kings 25:27,
28; [4]Ezek. 3:7–9; [5]Ezek., chap. 22; [6]Ezek., chap. 10; [7]Ezek.,
chap. 1; [8]Ezek., chap. 37; [9]Ezek., chap. 16; [10]Ezek., chap 17;
[11]Ezek., chap. 23; [12]Ezek., chaps. 4, 12; [13]Ezek. 24:15–27;
[14]Ezek. 33:21–33; [15]Ezek. 33:32, 33; [16]Ezek., chap. 18;

[17]Ezek. 14:13–20; [18]Ezek. 18:30–32; [19]Ezek., chaps. 38, 39; [20]Ezek. 10:1–22; 11:22–25.

2. When did Ezekiel begin to prophesy?

3. What new situation did he face?

4. In what form is his message cast?

5. What hope of success had he?

6. What was the "Vision of Ezekiel"?

7. What were some of his other great visions?

8. Into what three parts does the book fall?

9. How long did Ezekiel continue to prophesy?

10. What was the purpose of the new law in the closing chapters?

11. What important contribution did Ezekiel make to the Hebrew religion?

12. Why has he been called the Father of Judaism?

CHAPTER XI

THE BOOKS OF SAMUEL AND KINGS

It was about 1000 B.C. that David had been made king. In his reign of almost half a century Hebrew literature really began. There had long been songs and stories, sung or told from memory. But now men began to write them down, in the new script adapted from that of the Phoenicians, and before 900 the oft-told stories of tribal heroes like Saul and David were committed to writing.

It is of such materials, among others, that the work known to us as Samuel and Kings was made. It has come down to us as four books, but it forms a unit, and was finally shaped and organized by a single writer. But in his work he used, sometimes almost unaltered, sources so old that they must have been contemporary with the times they dealt with.

The most notable of these is the narrative that forms the core of the books of Samuel. So vivid, well informed, and objective is this story that it has been conjectured that it may actually be the work of David's lifelong friend Abiathar the priest, who was forced into retirement after the accession of Solomon, about 955 B.C.[1] One is tempted to imagine him in his old age beguiling his banishment at Anathoth by writing with unsparing candor the story of

68

the two kings, from the times of his forefather Eli to the death of David. His father Ahimelech had lost his life for giving David shelter, and Abiathar had fled to David when he was in the Cave of Adullam, and shared his fortunes thenceforth.[2] Certainly no one was in a better position to tell the story than he.

This is only a conjecture, of course, but it is certain that these narratives are masterpieces of the oriental story-teller's art, and historical materials of the utmost value and interest. David was the national hero of the Hebrews, and what we know of him is gained altogether from this absorbing narrative.

Hardly less important is the Northern Israel narrative of the deeds of the great northern prophets Elijah and Elisha, which was committed to writing about 800 B.C. or soon after.[3] Elijah possesses great importance for the history of Israel's religion because he advanced the doctrine that only the Lord God should be worshiped in Israel; all other deities should be rigidly excluded. This was an extreme position, for it was customary in the Orient for a new king to marry and take into his harem the daughters of friendly monarchs, and these women, like Solomon's Egyptian wife, or Ahab's wife Jezebel, naturally expected to continue to worship the gods of their fathers.

The book is a history, in something much better than the ancient manner, of the Hebrew monarchy, from its very beginnings to the bitter end. The narrative opens with the birth of Samuel, the kingmaker, and relates the hero stories about Saul and David, the glory of Solomon, the division of the kingdom, and the successive reigns that followed, until the Assyrians destroyed the Northern Kingdom in 721, and the Babylonians the Southern in 597 and 586. The last paragraph of all contains the pathetic account of how poor Jehoiachin, the boy of eighteen who had reigned three months and then been taken captive to Babylon, had in the thirty-seventh year of his captivity (561 B.C.) been released from prison and at last shown some consideration by his Babylonian masters.

This makes it very plain that this Book of Reigns was completed in the course of the Babylonian Exile, 597–538 B.C. It was based upon a variety of written sources which had grown up from David's time onward. The writer occasionally refers to such earlier works: the Book of the Records of Solomon;[4] the Book of the Chronicles of the Kings of Judah;[5] the Book of the Chronicles of the Kings of Israel.[6]

After the fall of the Northern Kingdom, its books were preserved and read in the Southern Kingdom of Judah. And there, out of such sources as these, some Jew of the seventh century before Christ, after the appearance of Deuteronomy, began to weave the old Judean and Ephraimitic narratives into an organized whole, approving or condemning the various kings as they appeared from his prophetic point of view. He was in deep sympathy with the Deuteronomic Law, which had come into force under Josiah in 621,[7] and traces of his attachment to it color his telling of the ancient story at many points. He shared the conviction, which Isaiah had expressed and Deuteronomy had encouraged, that God would never give Jerusalem up to its enemies.[8]

But these hopes were disappointed in the Babylonian conquest and the destruction of Jerusalem. And long after these events, some later Jewish exile solaced himself in his captivity, and in the midst of the national depression, by completing the story of the reigns, or kingdoms, with the overthrow of the Jewish monarchy and the two deportations, even down to the thirty-seventh year of the captivity of the ill-fated Jehoiachin, 561 B.C. It must therefore have been late in the Exile, and not long after that very date, that the book was completed.

In it we possess the framework of the main period of Jewish history, from the last days of the Judges to the midst of the Exile. This is enriched with many admirable narratives of the heroic times of Saul and David, and stirring scenes from the lives of Elijah and Elisha, the great prophets of the North. The whole is reviewed from the strongly prophetic point of view.

The man who gave final form to this great sketch of the Jewish state belonged to Judah and found more to approve in the history of the Southern Kingdom than in that of the Northern. Yet he felt that Judah, too, had sinned and deserved the misfortunes that had overtaken her. The history of the Northern Kingdom was indeed a terrible series of bloody usurpations. But in the south the Davidic line continued unbroken for four hundred years, and its restoration and perpetuation were the dream of the prophets of the Exile.

While the books of Samuel and Kings form one continuous narrative and received their present form from one writer, the Jews treated them as two books, Samuel and Kings. The Greek translators of the Hebrew Bible, in the third century before Christ, divided each of them into two parts, to accommodate them to the ordinary size of a convenient papyrus roll, calling them First, Second, Third, and Fourth Reigns or Kingdoms. Our names for them are a combination of the Greek and Hebrew systems.

Sixty years ago little more was known of the history of Western Asia than was afforded by the books of Samuel and Kings, supplemented by a few pages of Herodotus. But now the discoveries of the cuneiform records of Assyria and Babylonia have revealed the histories of those empires to us with a fulness even yet hardly realized. And these tablets and inscriptions also enable us to fill in the political and religious backgrounds of this history of the Hebrew kings and give us a new understanding of the conditions under which for a little more than four centuries the Jewish state endured.

SUGGESTIONS FOR STUDY

1. *References:* [1]I Kings 2:22–27; [2]I Sam., chap. 22; [3]I Kings 17:1—II Kings 13:21; [4]I Kings 11:41; [5]II Kings 21:25; [6]II Kings 10:34; [7]II Kings, chap. 22; [8]II Sam. 7:16; I Kings 9:3; 11:36; II Kings 8:19.

2. What is the scope of the books of Samuel and Kings?

3. Were they originally one, two, or four books?

4. From what point of view were they written?

5. What sources were used by the writer?

6. Through what stages has the work passed?

7. What is its relation to Deuteronomy?

8. When and where was it completed?

9. How did its author regard the Northern Kingdom?

10. How does he explain the overthrow of the Jewish state?

11. Who are the chief figures in the history of the united kingdom? Of the Northern Kingdom? Of the Southern Kingdom?

12. When did Hebrew literature begin?

13. What additional sources for the history are now available?

14. What military power destroyed the Northern Kingdom and when?

15. What military power destroyed the Southern Kingdom and when?

16. How does the writer contrive to tell the story of the two kingdoms simultaneously?

CHAPTER XII

THE BOOK OF JUDGES

The Exile made the full observance of the Deuteronomic Law impossible; the Temple was destroyed and the people were deported to Babylon. But much of that law was moral and personal in character, and thoughtful exiles were thrown back upon those sides of it which could still be obeyed. So strong was its influence upon them that they began to review their past history in the light of it and to recognize illustrations of its truth in the earlier experiences of the nation.

Among their books was one relating the exploits of their various tribal heroes in the confused and obscure period in the twelfth and eleventh centuries before Christ, when the Hebrews were struggling with the Canaanites and Philistines for the possession of the land. It was the story of one champion after another who arose in response to some pressing situation and for a while succeeded in leading and controlling his own tribe and its neighbors, for these tribal leaders did not command the support of all the tribes, which were only beginning to grope their way toward national consciousness.

Some of these stories were very ancient, and among them was included the oldest considerable piece of literature in the Old Testament, the War-Song of Deborah, which has been called the most important source in existence for the history of Israel, and probably comes from the twelfth century before Christ.[1] It begins with the Lord riding upon the storm from his home on Mount Sinai to aid his people in their battle, and exultingly describes the victory of the valiant tribes who rallied around Deborah and Barak to fight the Canaanite kings in the Plain of Esdraelon.[2] The book takes its name from these temporary leaders, who were called "judges" because the administration of some rude sort of justice was one of their duties. But those were times of violence and tumult, and it was the bold and shrewd soldier who usually made himself chief. Some of them were only names even to the ancient chronicler —Tola, Jair, Ibzan, Elon, Abdon. But about others clustered whole groups of legends like those connected with the name of Gideon, Jephthah, and Samson. Sometimes brutal, sometimes humorous, and always very primitive, these stories faithfully reflect the rough, wild, half-savage period with which they deal.

The Philistines, who were possessed of a somewhat developed civilization, had come over the sea perhaps from Crete, having been driven from their homes by barbarous Greek invaders, and had taken up their residence in Palestine. They had failed in an attempt to enter Egypt, but established themselves in the twelfth century before Christ along the seacoast of Palestine, which takes its name from them. The tribe of Dan came into collision with them, both claiming the desirable rolling country between the coast plain and the hills. Samson was the Danite champion and alternately fraternized with the Philistines and harried them.[3]

The Midianites, who belonged east of the Red Sea, came up through Moab and crossed the Jordan, into the Plain of Esdraelon. But Gideon mobilized the tribe of Manasseh against them and drove them back.[4] The Gileadites were harassed by the Ammonites, but taught them a severe lesson, under the leadership of Jephthah.[5] Their next quarrel was with their brothers the Ephraimites, against whom Jephthah again led them to victory.[6]

So one tribe fought another or its outside enemies generation after generation, through the days of the judges, and the tales of their warlike exploits, told over and over, were at length committed to writing and united into one book, probably in the seventh century before Christ. Then later, when the appearance of the Book of Deuteronomy had put such new spirit into Jewish religion, it was revised, probably in the course of the Exile, in accordance with the ideas of that book. It was at this time that the characteristic Deuteronomic framework was introduced: The Israelites did evil in the sight of the Lord, and he delivered them into the power of their enemies. Then they cried to the Lord and he sent them a deliverer. This was the Deuteronomic interpretation of the ceaseless ebb and flow of the period of the judges. This second form of the book contained substantially Judg. 2:6—16:31.

This prophetic edition was later enlarged by a writer of priestly sympathies, who prefaced it with an ancient summary of the conquest, 1:1—2:5, and added chapters 17–21. This took place after the writing of the priestly history, in the fifth century before Christ, which was to form the latest element in the Hexateuch. The Book of Judges was probably finished toward the end of the fifth century before Christ, seven hundred years after the composition of the Song of Deborah, which is the oldest part of it.

SUGGESTIONS FOR STUDY

1. *References:* [1]Judg., chap. 5; [2]Judg., chap. 4; [3]Judg., chaps. 13–16; [4]Judg. 6:1—8:28; [5]Judg. 10:6—11:40; [6]Judg. 12:1–7.

2. What period of history is dealt with in the Book of Judges?

3. What was the condition of the Hebrew people at that time?

4. Who were the leading figures of that period?

5. What was the character of their work?

6. Against what foes did Samson distinguish himself?

7. Against whom did Gideon lead the people?

8. Whom did Jephthah fight?

9. What is the theme of the Song of Deborah?

10. When were these stories first assembled in writing?

11. What influence did the Book of Deuteronomy exert upon them?

12. What final touches were put upon the book, and when was it finished?

13. What historical value has it?

14. What is its literary value?

CHAPTER XIII

THE BOOKS OF HAGGAI AND ZECHARIAH

One year in the life of the returned exiles is especially rich in prophecy and hence peculiarly well known to us. It is 520–519 B.C., when Haggai and Zechariah preached in Jerusalem. Darius had sent back more of the Jews to Palestine in 520, under the youthful Zerubbabel, the grandson of the unfortunate Jehoiachin, whom the exiles regarded as the last rightful king of Judah. It was eighteen years since Cyrus had sent the first party of returning exiles to Jerusalem, and now this second party had arrived. Yet no steps had been taken to rebuild the Temple; everybody was engrossed in his own affairs.

The wickedness of any longer putting off the rebuilding of the Temple stirred Haggai deeply, and very soon after the arrival of Zerubbabel and his company, he preached a sermon, calling upon Zerubbabel to undertake the work immediately. With Zerubbabel was associated Joshua, son of the last head of the old Jerusalem priesthood, and Haggai appealed to them both:

"Is it a time for you yourselves to live in your panelled houses, while this house lies waste?"[1]

We do not know who Haggai was, or whether he had come with Zerubbabel and had just arrived in Jerusalem. It is probable that he had. It was the twenty-eighth of September when he made this appeal, and Zerubbabel and Joshua led the people at once to the work of rebuilding.

But it was discouraging to see how little they could accomplish in comparison with the old Temple that the Babylonians had destroyed sixty-six years before. Not quite two months later Haggai once more addressed them.

"Who is there left among you that saw this house in its ancient splendor? And how it looks to you now! Does it not seem to you like nothing at all? . . . . Be strong . . . . and work; for I am with you, ... and I will fill this house with splendor; . . . . the future splendor of this house shall be greater than the past, and upon this place I will bestow prosperity."[2]

Two months more passed and early in 519 B.C. Haggai preached again. It was the twenty-fourth day of the ninth month. If they have not prospered, said the prophet, it is because they have been unclean in the sight of God. But now, with the Temple rebuilding, and the sacrifice worthily offered, if they will hold aloof from defiling contacts with their unclean neighbors, a new era of well-being will dawn for them, beginning from that very day.[3]

On the same day Haggai preached another sermon, his fourth and last, so far as we know. The
kingdoms of the nations are to be shaken, but God
has chosen Zerubbabel, and he shall be a "seal-ring"
—a symbol of the highest significance and distinction.[4] These four messages of Haggai all deal with
the rebuilding of the Temple in Jerusalem, and they
fall within four months.

Two months after Haggai's first sermon, and so
toward the close of 520, Zechariah began his preaching. He reminded the returned exiles that God had
warned their forefathers, and all that the prophets
had threatened them with had come to pass. They,
in their turn, must heed his warnings, if they wish
to avoid his anger.[5]

Two months after Haggai's last sermon Zechariah preached again to the exiles, assuring them that
the Temple should be rebuilt and God would again
favor them:

> "I will return to Jerusalem in mercy;
> My house shall be rebuilt therein; . . . .
> The Lord will again have pity upon Zion,
> And again choose Jerusalem."[6]

Zechariah's prophecy was of the apocalyptic
type, of which we have seen the beginnings in Ezekiel. The vision of the horseman among the myrtle
trees, the four horns, the measuring line, the lamp
and the olive trees, the flying roll, the woman in the

measure, and the four chariots teach the purification and protection of the land and the future glory of the city. Who has despised a day of small things? Jerusalem is to be so great and populous that it will be impossible to inclose it with a wall. Aged men and women shall again be seen in Jerusalem:

"And the streets of the city shall be filled
    With boys and girls, playing in its streets."[7]

Zechariah sought to cheer his struggling companions with the hope of Israel's messianic destiny: "In those days, ten men, from nations of every language, shall lay hold of him who is a Jew, saying, 'Let us go with you; for we have heard that God is with you!' "[8]

So the new Temple was completed, and the old worship was at last resumed.

To the ancient collection that contained the preaching of Zechariah, chapters 1–8, other kindred prophecies from later times have been added. A mention of Greece,[9] combined with allusions to the captivity and the Dispersion and frequent use of the writings of earlier prophets, shows that these are the work of later hands. They echo and enlarge upon Zechariah's bright hopes for the future. Jerusalem is at last to be a truly holy city; the very bells of the horses will be marked "Holy to the Lord."[10] And, best of all, the Messiah is to come and bring in his peaceful reign:

Exult greatly, O daughter of Zion,
Shout with joy, O daughter of Jerusalem.
Lo, your king comes to you;
Vindicated and victorious is he;
Humble, and riding upon an ass,
Even upon a colt, the foal of an ass. . . . .
He shall command peace upon the nations.
His dominion shall be from sea to sea,
And from the river to the ends of the earth.[11]

SUGGESTIONS FOR STUDY

1. *References:* [1]Hag. 1:4; [2]Hag. 2:3-9; [3]Hag. 2:15-19; [4]Hag. 2:23; [5]Zech. 1:2-6; [6]Zech. 1:16, 17; [7]Zech. 8:4, 5; [8]Zech. 8:23; [9]Zech. 9:13; [10]Zech. 14:20; [11]Zech. 9:9, 10.

2. What situation stirred Haggai and Zechariah to preach?

3. When did they prophesy?

4. How much time does the preaching of Haggai, as we know it, cover?

5. What was its effect?

6. What form did the preaching of Zechariah take?

7. What were his hopes for the city and nation?

8. What hopes color the later oracles of chaps. 9 ff.?

CHAPTER XIV

THE BOOK OF MALACHI

Half a century after the rebuilding of the Temple in 516 B.C. religious conditions at Jerusalem were very distressing. The ritual was carried on in a slovenly and mechanical fashion. The priests were as lax in teaching the Law as they were in obeying it. The people offered their poorest instead of their best animals in sacrifice, and withheld the tithes they were supposed to pay for the support of the worship. They were divorcing their Jewish wives and marrying women not of Jewish blood. All sorts of vulgar vices prevailed.

All this roused a prophet of the fifth century to try to stir his people out of their lethargy and baseness. His name is forgotten, but his prophecy, once an appendix to Zechariah, has come down to us under the name of Malachi, from the occurrence of that word, meaning "My Messenger," in chapter 3:

"Behold, I will send forth my messenger,
    And he shall prepare the way before me!"[1]

Malachi—for we have no other name for him—rebukes the priests and the people for their perfunctory and half-hearted service and their miserable offerings.[2] They seem to think very lightly of their God. And he, for his part, would prefer to have the

Temple closed and the service cease than to have it carried on in this careless, uninterested fashion. For he is not dependent upon them:

"For from the rising of the sun, even to its setting,
    My name is great among the nations;
    And in every place an offering is made, is brought
        near to my name,
    And a pure offering.
    For my name is great among the nations."[3]

This acceptance on the part of God of heathen worship, when it is sincerely offered, no matter whether under Jewish forms or not, shows us once more how the prophets were constantly breaking through even in the most unpromising times to the great realities of ethical religion.

The denunciation of divorce[4] may be quite as much intended as a warning against giving up the old religion and accepting a new one. Like every oracle in Malachi, it has some lines that are unforgettable:

Have we not all one father?
Did not one God create us? . . . .
So take heed to your spiritual life,
And let nobody be faithless to the wife of his
    youth.[5]

The people in their wickedness have forgotten the justice of God. But his Judgment Day is surely coming:[6]

"Behold, I will send forth my messenger,
    And he shall prepare the way before me! . . . .
    And who can endure the day of his coming?
    And who can stand when he appears?
    For he shall be like a refiner's fire,
    And like fullers' soap . . . .
    And shall cleanse the sons of Levi."[7]

It was this prophecy of the coming of the Angel of the Covenant to usher in the Great Repentance that was afterward understood of John the Baptist.

In most vigorous terms Malachi calls upon the people to pay their tithes:[8]

"Bring the whole tithe into the storehouse . . . .
    And see if I will not open for you the windows of
        the heavens
    And pour out for you a blessing until there is no
        more need."[9]

Malachi's little book closes with mingled warning and encouragement:[10]

"You say, 'It is useless to serve God;
    And what profit is it that we have kept his charge,
    And that we have walked in mourning before the
        Lord of Hosts?
    And now we are deeming the arrogant fortunate;
    The doers of wickedness, indeed, are built up;
    They test God, also, and they escape!' "[11]

The prophet assures them that God has not forgotten them; a book of remembrance has been written concerning them and they will be God's special treasure. His judgment against the wicked is sure to come:

"But for you who revere my name, there will arise
The sun of righteousness, with healing in its
wings."[12]

Malachi gives us an authentic glimpse of Jewish life in a half-ruinous and utterly discouraged Jerusalem, and helped to prepare the way for Nehemiah, who came in 444 B.C., to rebuild its walls.

SUGGESTIONS FOR STUDY

1. *References:* [1]Mal. 3:1; [2]Mal. 1:6—2:9; [3]Mal. 1:11; [4]Mal. 2:10-16; [5]Mal. 2:10, 15; [6]Mal. 2:17—3:5; [7]Mal. 3:1-3; [8]Mal. 3:6-12; [9]Mal. 3:10; [10]Mal. 3:13—4:5; [11]Mal. 3:14, 15; [12]Mal. 4:2.

2. What is the origin of the name Malachi?

3. When and where was the book written?

4. What was the condition of the Temple at that time?

5. What was the state of Jewish religion?

6. What abuses are especially attacked by Malachi?

7. What great religious truth did he utter?

8. What other Old Testament prophets show hostility to Edom? (1:2–5).

9. What was the ground of this bitterness?

10. What is the relation of Malachi to Zechariah? Compare Mal. 1:1 with Zech. 12:1.

11. What has the Book of Malachi to offer for modern religious life?

CHAPTER XV

THE BOOK OF OBADIAH

The kingdom of Judah was ringed about by hereditary enemies, and when it was conquered and Jerusalem fell, they rejoiced in its downfall. Especially Edom, to the southeast, showed indecent haste in co-operating with Judah's conquerors and harassing her fugitives. They joined in the pillage of the city and afterward appropriated what they could get of the Judean territory.

This graceless inhumanity stirred the indignation of the prophet Obadiah. He speaks almost like a participant in some of the scenes he describes, but he can hardly have witnessed them as he reflects the condition of Edom a century later, when the Arabs were already dispossessing the Edomites:

> "The men who were at peace with you have overpowered you.
> Your associates have put a foreign people in your place."[1]

The Edomites had gloated over the Jews in their adversity; they had laughed at their trouble. They had cut off the fugitives and betrayed the refugees. They had shared in the plunder of the stricken city when it could no longer protect itself. Obadiah draws a striking picture of the vulture-like behavior of Edom, glad to devour the prey that bolder peoples had brought down. When Esau should have come to the support of his brother Jacob, he had basely sided against him instead.[2]

All this reflects the atmosphere of the destruction of Jerusalem by Nebuchadnezzar in 586 B.C. and the subsequent aggressions of the Edomites. Ezekiel says of them in the days of the Exile: "In the fire of my indignation I speak against the rest of the nations, and especially against Edom—the whole of it—who with malicious glee and bitter contempt took over my land as a possession for themselves, to hold it as a prey."[3]

Edom had seized the opportunity to take possession of a good part of Judah's former territory. But she herself was soon to feel like pressure from the south. She trusted in her mountainous situation and her rocky retreats—

> "You who dwell in the clefts of the cliff,
>   And set your dwelling on high,
>   And say to yourself,
>   'Who can bring me down to the earth?' "[4]

But against her in the sixth century were already moving the Arabs of the southern desert, who eventually, in 312 B.C., actually captured her capital Petra, with its rock-hewn palaces. Something of this dawning peril was known to Obadiah, and he sees in

it the inevitable judgment of God for Edom's crimes
against Judah:

> "Though you build your nest high like the eagle,
>   And set your nest even among the stars,
>   From there I will bring you down."[5]

Edom is to be pillaged in its turn:

> "How Esau is ransacked,
>   And his treasures plundered!
>   They have cast you forth to the boundary,
>   All those who were in league with you have be-
>   trayed you."
> "In that day,"—it is the oracle of the Lord,—
> "I will certainly destroy the wise men from Edom,
>   And intelligence from Mount Esau. . . . .
>   For the violence done to your brother Jacob,
>   Shame shall cover you and you shall be cut off
>   forever."[6]

This will be but a part of the dreadful Day of the
Lord, when judgment shall overtake the nations,
Edom with the rest:

> "As you have done, it shall be done to you,
>   Your deed shall return upon your own head."[7]

A considerable displacement of Edomites by
Arabs from the south took place in the fifth century
before Christ, and this is probably the time when
Obadiah wrote his bitter reproach of Edom. With

his wrath against it and the other nations is coupled hope for the future supremacy of Judah and the utter destruction of Edom:

"The house of Jacob shall be a fire,
  And the house of Joseph a flame;
  And the house of Esau shall be stubble,
  And they shall lick them up and devour them;
  And there shall be no survivor to the house of
    Esau."
  For the Lord has spoken.[8]

Like Jeremiah before him, Obadiah used as the text[9] for his invective against Edom the words of some older prophet, which appear also in Jer. 49:14–16, 9 f. and 7. We might suppose Obadiah was here quoting Jeremiah, if it were not that the verses stand in a more natural and original order in Obadiah than in Jeremiah. His bitter outcry against Edom has a number of parallels in Old Testament prophecy. There was the unknown prophet from whom Jeremiah was quoting, in 49:7–22. There was Jeremiah himself; there was the oracle against Edom that has found a place in Amos 1:11, 12; and there was the prophecy of the hideous day of vengeance upon Edom that forms the thirty-fourth chapter of Isaiah. So hatred of Edom forms a dark thread in the pattern of Hebrew religious thought in the sixth and fifth centuries before Christ.

SUGGESTIONS FOR STUDY

1. *References:* [1]Obad. 1:7; [2]Obad. 1:10–14; [3]Ezek. 36:5; [4]Obad. 1:3; [5]Obad. 1:4; [6]Obad. 1:6–10; [7]Obad. 1:15; [8]Obad. 1:18; [9]Obad. 1:1–9.

2. What is the subject of the prophecies of Obadiah?

3. When did he prophesy?

4. What other prophets dealt with the same subject?

5. What had so stirred their indignation?

6. What is the explanation of the resemblance of 1:1–9 to Jer. 49:7–22?

7. What force was at this time pressing upon Edom and what later resulted from it?

CHAPTER XVI

THE BOOK OF JOEL

The mysterious Book of Joel reveals a desperate condition of things among the Jews. They are a little religious community—the "congregation"—gathered about the rebuilt Temple, headed by priests and elders instead of kings, and subject to the Persian Empire. Now the locusts have settled upon the land and eaten up the crops, until there is neither food nor fodder. To their ravages are added the horrors of drought. Famine confronts man and beast. So great is the scarcity that even the daily offering at the Temple that united the congregation with its God has had to be given up. The people are so impoverished that some of them have actually sold their children to the Philistine slave-dealers, to be carried off to the Greek west.[1] Even today such things happen in desperate times in Asia.

It was this situation that roused Joel, about 400 B.C., to utter the brief prophecies by which we know him. He was steeped in the prophetic literature of his people; the works of a dozen earlier Jewish writers are reflected in his few pages. He draws a powerful picture of the plague and the drought. There has never been anything like it:

What the shearer left, the locust ate;
And what the locust left, the hopper ate;
And what the hopper left, the destroyer ate.[2]

Joel summons the people to fasting and prayer:

Return to the Lord your God;
For he is gracious and merciful, ...
Assemble the people; order a holy congregation.

Let the priests, the ministers of the Lord, weep,
And let them say, "Spare thy people, O Lord!"[3]

The longed-for relief came:

The Lord became solicitous for his land,
And had pity upon his people.[4]

Hope revived, and the peril passed. The early and the later rains came down as of old.

Joel saw in the plague of locusts a portent of the awful Day of the Lord of which the prophets so often spoke. They had come over the land like an invading army:

They look like horses,
And they run like war-horses . . . .
Like a mighty people
Arrayed for battle.[5]

The Day was to be a day of darkness and gloom, a day of clouds and deep darkness. But after the people's repentance and God's forgiveness, it takes on a brighter aspect:

"It shall come to pass afterward,
  That I will pour out my spirit upon all flesh;
  Your sons and your daughters shall prophesy;
  Your old men shall dream dreams,
  And your young men shall see visions."[6]

But Joel still, like the prophets of old, denounces vengeance upon the heathen. God will gather the nations into the neighboring valley of Jehoshaphat ("Jehovah Judges") for judgment.

      There will I sit to judge
      All the nations from every side.
      For the harvest is ripe! . . . .
      For the wine-press is full! . . . .
      For their wickedness is great.[7]

A golden age to come still beckons the prophet's hope. God is again to dwell in Zion, his holy mountain. Jerusalem shall be holy, and inviolable once more:

"Egypt shall become a waste,
  And Edom shall be a barren steppe; . . . .
  But Judah shall abide forever,
  And Jerusalem for generation after generation."[8]

With such dreams of a great future for his people and his religion Joel reanimated the little Jewish community in one of the darkest hours of its later history. He was a striking embodiment of that indomitable spiritual hope that was the soul of Judaism.

SUGGESTIONS FOR STUDY

1. *References:* [1]Joel 3:3, 6; [2]Joel 1:4; [3]Joel 2:13, 16, 17; [4]Joel 2:18; [5]Joel 2:4, 5; [6]Joel 2:28; [7]Joel 3:12, 13; [8]Joel 3:19, 20.

2. What situation is reflected in the Book of Joel?

3. What great idea of Amos and Zephaniah did this recall to his mind?

4. What did Joel call upon the priests and people to do?

5. What followed?

6. What further picture of the future came to his mind?

7. What is Joel's view of the heathen and their destiny?

8. What are his hopes for Judah and Jerusalem?

CHAPTER XVII

THE BOOK OF RUTH

The return of the exiles created new and serious problems. Some of the Jews had married women not of Jewish descent. These mixed marriages were sternly condemned by Ezra the Scribe, about 397 B.C., who obliged such men to divorce these wives and put away the children they had had by them.[1] He felt that the nation had suffered terribly for its former laxity in religious matters, and long residence in heathen and hence "unclean" lands had intensified in him the traditional Jewish aversion to foreigners.

This harsh action naturally caused great unhappiness and injustice. Over against Ezra and his strict and rigorous policy many people held that in religion there were other things that counted quite as much as pure Jewish descent. Loyalty, piety, and goodness were acceptable to God in other people besides Jews.

In this spirit of protest the Book of Ruth was written. It is an idyllic story. The scene is laid in the time of the Judges. Driven by famine, a man of Bethlehem with his wife and his sons moved eastward into Moab, where he died. There his sons married women of Moab, and there they afterward died.

Their mother Naomi prepared to return to Bethlehem, and her daughters-in-law set out with her.[2] But she bade them remain in their own country, and one of them did so. The other, Ruth, would not leave her and insisted upon going with her to Bethlehem:

"Do not press me to leave you," she said, "to turn back from following you; for wherever you go, I will go; and wherever you lodge, I will lodge; your people shall be my people, and your god my god; wherever you die, I will die, and there will I be buried. May the Lord requite me and worse, if even death separate me from you."[3]

Arrived in Bethlehem, Ruth was allowed to gather what barley the reapers left in the field of Boaz, a rich relative of Naomi's husband. Under the Jewish law, a man's widow should be married by his brother or his next of kin. In view of this, Naomi instructed Ruth to approach Boaz as he slept in the field after the threshing and claim her right to become his wife. Boaz acknowledged her claim, and after the proper formalities before the elders of the city he married her. Their son became the grandfather of David.[4]

So out of the memory of a Moabite strain in the ancestry of David came this story of the devotion and piety of a Moabite girl to her Jewish mother-in-law. If the children of such marriages were unclean in the sight of Ezra, what of David himself, whose grandfather was the child of just such a mixed marriage? And were not women like Ruth worthy to stand with the women of Israel?

The breadth and understanding of the Book of Ruth make it stand out against the narrow exclusiveness of its times, and the naturalness of its simple yet vivid style marks it as one of the gems of Hebrew literature. Even in the midst of the legalism that was already beginning to stifle Judaism, there were some who could see, as Paul did long after, that the real Jew is not one who is so outwardly; the real Jew is the one who is so inwardly, whose praise is not from men but from God.

SUGGESTIONS FOR STUDY

1. *References:* [1]Ezra 9:1—10:17; [2]Ruth 1:1-7; [3]Ruth 1:16, 17; [4]Ruth, chaps. 2-4.

2. What is the story of Ruth?

3. In what time is the scene laid?

4. What situation called it forth?

5. How did it apply to the situation?

6. What is its literary quality?

7. How did Paul afterward express its fundamental idea?

8. What serious and lasting consequences did the harsh policy as to mixed marriages have? See Neh. 13:28; Josephus, *Antiquities* xi.8.2.

9. Why does the book stand next after Judges in the Bible?

CHAPTER XVIII

THE BOOK OF JOB

Hebrew literature is rich in varied forms of expression, but it developed no great drama. The nearest approach to it is the Book of Job, which may be described as a drama without action. It is in substance a discussion of the old problem of suffering in human life. What is its cause? What is its meaning? Why do upright people suffer? But the book makes so little real contribution to that subject that it is perhaps truer to say that its purpose is to correct the current notion that disaster and misfortune are tokens of God's disapproval of one's sins, while prosperity and good fortune are signs of his approbation and favor.

Ezekiel speaks of Job as a conspicuously righteous man, along with Noah and Daniel,[1] and his vague figure has been made the hero of this parable of human experience.

The germ of the book, which is probably older than the rest, is formed by the prologue, chapters 1 and 2, and the epilogue, 42:7–16, which tell the story of Job, a patriarch of Edom, perfectly upright and yet pursued by misfortune until he is almost driven to despair. Into this older narrative a Hebrew philosopher early in the fourth century before

Christ introduced the speeches by Job and his three friends which form the main part of the book.

It is a terrible thing to endure misfortune which you have done nothing to incur, and doubly so when all the world interprets it as a just punishment for some sin you have committed. This was the ancient attitude to calamity, and must have greatly embittered the lot of many godly and upright people who were overtaken by misfortune. It is against this cheap view of suffering that the Book of Job is directed.

The poet-philosopher who first expanded this sought to describe the thoughts of Job and of his three friends who had come to comfort him in his misery. Perhaps their long seven-day silence led Job to think that they were in their hearts taking the conventional view of his condition. At any rate it is Job who at length breaks the silence. He laments that he was ever born, and from the first sentence you know that you are in the presence of one of the world's greatest poets.

Job is answered by his first friend, Eliphaz, who voices the common view of adversity: "Who that was innocent ever perished? . . . . Those who plow guilt and sow sorrow, reap it . . . . Can a mortal man be righteous before God? . . . . Man is born for trouble, even as sparks fly upward!"[2] But there is more than pessimism or mere resignation in the speech of Eliphaz:

"I, however, would seek for God,
  And to God I would state my case."[3]

And there is a meaning and a discipline in suffering, for the man who accepts it in the right spirit:

"Happy . . . . is the man whom God reproves,
  So do not reject the instruction of the Almighty."[4]

Job answers bitterly, hurt by his friend's easy assumption of his guilt.[5]

His second friend, Bildad, then speaks, urging Job to seek God in his distress:

"If you yourself would seek God, ...
  If you were but pure and straight,
  Then, indeed, he would bestir himself in your behalf."[6]

Bildad, too, is of the conventional school but he holds out some hope to Job:

"God will not reject a perfect man, ...
  He will yet fill your mouth with laughter,
  And your lips with shouting."[7]

Job answers in a passage of the profoundest pathos.[8] He is conscious of no fault, yet how can he hope to convince God? He has that terrible feeling of abandonment. God has departed from him; he knows not why. His third friend, Zophar, then speaks, rebuking Job,[9] and Job bursts forth in scornful invective against them all:

"No doubt but you are the people,
   And wisdom will die with you! . . . .
I know that I am innocent" . . . .

"Wherefore dost thou hide thy face,
   And reckon me as thy foe?
Wilt thou scare a driven leaf,
   And chase the dry stubble?"[10]

This concludes the first cycle of the great debate.
The second is opened by Eliphaz, whom Job answers. Bildad speaks again and Job replies. Zophar
continues the argument and Job answers him, completing the second cycle. The third cycle follows the
same course: Eliphaz, Job; Bildad, Job; Zophar,
Job, for 27:7-23 and perhaps also chapter 28, the
poem in praise of Wisdom, should probably be understood as Zophar's third speech. In his final
speech in his debate with his friends Job eloquently
contrasts his former felicity with his present wretch-
edness:

"Oh that I were as in months of old,
   As in the days when God guarded me . . . .
When the friendship of God was over my tent,
   When the Almighty was still with me! . . . .
But now they laugh at me,
   Those who are younger than I,
Whose fathers I disdained
   To set with the dogs of my flock."[11]

Then in a series of great stanzas Job protests his
innocence of one sin after another. He has always
abstained from evil and given himself to good; why
has God forsaken him?

"Here is my signature! Let the Almighty answer
  me!" . . . .
The words of Job are finished.[12]

Then the Lord answered Job from the whirlwind,
saying:

"Who is this that obscures counsel
  By words without knowledge? . . . .
Where were you when I laid the foundations of
  the earth? . . . .
Who fixed its measurements,—for you should
  know? . . . .
Or who laid its corner stone,
When the morning stars sang together,
And all the gods shouted for joy? . . . .
Have you ever in your life commanded the morn-
  ing? . . . .
Have you gone to the sources of the sea? . . . .
Can you bind the chains of the Pleiades,
Or loosen the girdle of Orion?"[13]

Job acknowledges his utter insignificance: "What
can I answer thee?"[14] God speaks again, declaring
his incomparable might, and Job acknowledges his
own ignorance and dulness:

"I had heard of thee by the hearing of the ear,
  But now my eye has seen thee.

Therefore I retract and repent
In dust and ashes."[15]

In the end Job's problem is left unsolved, except
that in the infinite wisdom of God undeserved suffering must have an explanation beyond our com-
prehension. This is, after all, the simple doctrine of
faith, which does not insist upon explaining everything, but trusts the fundamental love and care of
God in prosperity and adversity alike. It is not
stated in Job in terms of Christian warmth and love
but it is nevertheless there. Job's inward experience
of God at last satisfies him that there is a deeper justice and a deeper meaning in life than we can sometimes see. God speaks to him and he is satisfied.
It is not mere misfortune that has staggered him, it
is the agonizing delusion that God has abandoned
him.

To a later Hebrew poet it seemed wrong that Job
should thus triumph in the debate over his conventional friends, and he introduced the four speeches
by Elihu that immediately follow Job's agonized appeal to God.[16] They present over again the old popular Jewish view that misfortune is the punishment
of sin, but with far less power and genius than the
original author possessed. They also destroy the
symmetry of the poem and defeat its dramatic
movement, for they separate God's answer from
Job's impassioned appeal, which logically and emo-
tionally it directly follows. For at the end of chapter 31 Job is clearly waiting for God to answer him,

and God's first words in 38:2—"Who is this that
obscures counsel by words without knowledge?"—
unmistakably refer to Job. The interpolated chapters add little to what the three friends had already
said, and their literary quality must strike every
reader as inferior to that of the rest of the book. If
Job was written about 400 B.C., they were probably
added a century or more later.

SUGGESTIONS FOR STUDY

1. *References:* [1]Ezek. 14:14, 20; [2]Job 4:7, 8, 17; 5:7;
[3]Job 5:8; [4]Job 5:17; [5]Job 6:1—7:21; [6]Job 8:5, 6; [7]Job 8:20,
21; [8]Job 9:1—10:22; [9]Job 11:1-20; [10]Job 12:1; 13:18, 24,
25; [11]Job 29:2, 4, 5; 30:1; [12]Job 31:35, 40; [13]Job 38:1, 2, 4-7,
12, 16, 31; [14]Job 40:4; [15]Job 42:5, 6; [16]Job, chaps. 32-37.

2. What was the conventional view of misfortune and
suffering among the Jews?

3. What change in this does the Book of Job seek to
make?

4. What three stages can be traced in the growth of the
book?

5. What is the literary quality of the book?

6. What parts of it contain the noblest poetry?

7. What is the aim of the Elihu speeches?

8. What is chap. 28?

9. What attitude toward the problem is taken in Ps. 22?

10. What light do the suffering and death of Christ
throw upon it?

11. What attitude is expressed in Henley's *Invictus?*

12. What is the Christian attitude toward misfortune and
suffering?

13. Is it identical with that of Job or of his friends?

14. Did the Book of Job prepare the way for it?

CHAPTER XIX

THE HEXATEUCH

The most commanding work of Hebrew genius sprang not out of the years of national power and prestige but out of the days of obscurity and depression that followed the return from exile. It is that great body of history, tradition, and law that we know as the Hexateuch—the books of Genesis, Exodus, Leviticus, Numbers, Deuteronomy, and Joshua. It was completed not long after 400 B.C., but it arose from sources and forces many centuries older.

The oldest of these elements was a Judean account of the nation's story from the beginning of the world to the conquest of Canaan by the tribes. It was the first sustained history to be written anywhere. The writer of it believed that the march of events was simply the working-out of divine purposes. Babylonian myths and legends and Canaanite popular tales he freely appropriated to his great purpose of enforcing morality and the worship of one God. Sometimes crude old superstitious ideas still cling to some of these.

The writer of this ancient record was a prophet, and told the story from the prophet's point of view. He wrote his book about 850 B.C. in the Southern Kingdom of Judah.

A hundred years later, in the Northern Kingdom of Israel, another prophetic writer gathered up the thrice-told tales of his world into a great historical narrative. It began with the story of Abraham, but its masterpiece was the story of Joseph. It is more tender and scrupulous than its great predecessor of Judah, as we might expect in the times of the prophet Amos. The writer was influenced by the work of Elijah, the great prophet of the North, and was controlled by the idea that Israel must serve God alone.

After the fall of the Northern Kingdom before Assyria in 721 B.C., its literature passed into southern hands, where the great Judean history had so long been current. It was inevitable that the two narratives, so alike in religious interest and so often parallel in material, should be combined, and this was done in Judah, in the course of the seventh century before Christ, the last century of the Judean kingdom. In this work Hebrew prose reached its highest level.

In that same period, as we have seen, when reaction under the half-heathen king Manasseh drove the prophets into hiding, they produced the Book of Deuteronomy.[1] This, with the new history just described, the Jews carried with them into captivity, after the disasters of 597 and 586 B.C. And in the captivity in Babylonia these books were combined into a great composite work of history and law, all conceived from a fundamentally prophetic point of view.

The Exile was a time of great literary activity on the part of the Jews. Faced with the collapse of their national fortunes, they seem to have found their literary heritage all the more precious, and to have sought in every way to preserve and enhance it. They were, moreover, dreaming of a return to their own land and devising means to prevent the recurrence of the catastrophe that had plunged them into exile.

They now felt that their desolation was caused by their failure to please God and serve him faithfully, and to safeguard the nation in the future and insure its holiness, priestly exiles like Ezekiel produced the temple legislation of Ezekiel, chapters 40–48, and the still earlier Holiness Code of Leviticus, chapters 17–26, written probably between 597 and 586, with its undertone: "You must be holy, for I, the Lord your God, am holy."[2] Their ideal was theocratic; God himself was to be the head of the state in the future. The nation was to exclude from itself all unclean heathen elements, and devote itself wholly to the service and the worship of God.

In such a spirit, after the Exile, priestly authors created a new history. It began with a majestic account of the Creation, which was represented as culminating in the institution of the Jewish Sabbath.[3] Its narrative was supplemented with painstaking genealogies—for purity of Jewish blood had assumed religious importance—and accounts of tribal arrangements, and especial attention was given to matters of law and religious ceremonial. There was a covenant relation of the most solemn kind between Israel and God, and this underlay the whole religious practice of the nation.

This great expression of the priestly conception of religion and its institutions was completed toward the middle of the fifth century before Christ, taking its place beside the great older prophetic book of history and law which had taken shape about the Book of Deuteronomy. The new work was probably the textbook of Ezra's reforms of 397 B.C. The two works were so parallel and so supplementary that they were soon combined into a single whole, preserving and as far as possible adjusting and harmonizing the leading features and materials of both.

So at last, not long after 400 B.C., arose the Hexateuch. The extraordinary thing about it is its scope, for it seeks to unify and organize the whole range of human history, society, institutions, law, and religion. It was a cosmogony, an outline of history, an account of human origins and social institutions, a system of worship, and a handbook of religion and morals—all rolled in one. It would be difficult to find in the world's literature any parallel to the sweep of this tremendous work, into which some great Jew late in the Persian period wrought the diverse literary inheritance of his nation.

The literary problem presented by the Hexateuch and its sources is one of the most intricate in the whole range of literature. But it may be substantially summarized as follows: The Judean history arose about 850 B.C.; the Ephraimitic history, about 750 B.C.; they were combined in the following century, before the publication of Deuteronomy in 621 B.C., and presumably before its composition, perhaps about 650 B.C.; in the following century, 600–500 B.C., this joint history was in turn united with Deuteronomy; late in the fifth century the priestly book of history and law was written, and early in the fourth century, or soon after 400 B.C., this too was united by priestly hands with the great corpus of ancient history and law that had thus grown up, to form substantially what we know as Genesis to Joshua. The Hexateuch was therefore almost five hundred years in the making.

This work, which by itself is almost as long as the whole New Testament, was a single book, but it was soon divided into six parts, which we know by the Greek names given them when they were translated into Greek, in Egypt in the third century before Christ: Genesis (Beginning); Exodus (Going Out); Leviticus (the Levitical Book); Numbers (from the Numbering of the People, chaps. 1–4, 26); Deuteronomy (the Second Giving of the Law), and Joshua (the hero of the sixth book).

The reverence with which Deuteronomy had been regarded from the time of its discovery gradually extended to all the books that preceded it in the Hexateuch, and these five, Genesis–Deuteronomy, came to be called the Law and formed the core about which the rest of the Hebrew scriptures, the Prophets and the Writings, later gathered.

SUGGESTIONS FOR STUDY

1. *References:* [1]Chap. vii; [2]Lev. 19:2; [3]Gen., chap. 1.

2. What is the Hexateuch?

3. Compare the priestly account of creation (Gen. 1:1—2:3) with the prophetic account (Gen. 2:4–25).

4. What are the four main sources of the Hexateuch?

5. When did each of them arise?

6. Through what stages of combination did they pass?

7. What is the scope of the narrative of the Hexateuch?

8. What part of it reflects the work of Ezekiel?

9. What part of it did Ezra urge upon the people?

10. To what part of it do we owe the story of Joseph?

11. What social institutions does it explain?

12. What has it to say about the beginnings of arts and crafts?

13. What explanation does it offer for the unity and harmony of nature? What other explanations occur to you?

14. What are some of its characteristic religious and social attitudes? (Cf. Lev., 11; 19:18; 20:27; 24:20.)

15. How did the makers of our present six books divide the materials of the Hexateuch?

16. What do you consider the most important and significant portions of each book?

CHAPTER XX

THE BOOK OF JONAH

The Jewish prophets thought of their nation as peculiarly chosen and favored by God, and yet they saw the world controlled generation after generation by cruel heathen powers. The chosen people, as they considered themselves, were conquered and scattered, and the prophets denounced and condemned their conquerors in strong and bitter terms. Yet the nation did not recover, but fell into a state of settled insignificance and impotence. Assyria, Egypt, Babylon, and Persia dominated it one after the other, and the proud claims and high hopes of Judaism seemed farther from fulfilment than ever. For the few who still cherished those claims and hopes, the religious adjustment to all this disappointment and humiliation was indescribably hard.

At length it dawned upon the Jewish mind that there was a nobler solution of the great enigma than the old familiar one of meeting hatred with hatred and bitterness with bitterness. That had risen out of the old narrow way of conceiving God as peculiarly their own, and supremely concerned with their welfare. But suppose he really cared for other nations and peoples just as much as he cared for the Jews? That would put the whole matter in a different perspective.

Of course the way had been prepared for this by the sublime ethical monotheism of the earliest literary prophets, and by Jeremiah's doctrine of religion as an individual matter and Ezekiel's teaching of personal responsibility. Ezekiel had seen that God took no pleasure in the death of the wicked: "I have no pleasure in the death of the wicked, but rather in this, that the wicked man turn from his way and live."[1]

But Ezekiel had said this of the Jews: "Why should you die, O household of Israel?"[2] It remained for a later prophet, about the middle of the fourth century before Christ, to rise to the splendid thought that this was as true of the heathen as of the Jews, and that God as creator had the same concern, the same forbearance and compassion, for all his creatures, whether Jew or Gentile.

Such a teaching was particularly timely after the days of Ezra, when Jewish life became so permeated with narrowness and arrogance. It was to correct that harsh and unlovely attitude in late Judaism that the Book of Jonah was written. The followers of Ezra had gone to one extreme, but the position in which it left them was religiously intolerable. It filled the heart with bitterness instead of peace. The true remedy must lie in the very opposite direction; in the direction of breadth, sympathy, and love, even for one's enemies. This is the most difficult of all lessons, and the most indispensable.

This is the message of the Book of Jonah. Jonah,

the son of Amittai, was a Galilean prophet of the eighth century before Christ; he is mentioned in II Kings.[3] Four hundred years later he was made the hero of a story or parable to teach the great new lesson that, as Paul afterward said, God does not belong to the Jews alone; he belongs to the heathen also.[4]

Jonah is called by God to go to Nineveh, the Assyrian capital, and preach against it, but instead of obeying he flees in the opposite direction, and takes passage in a ship for Tarshish, to get away from the presence of the Lord. His amazing adventures on the voyage make up the best-known story in the Bible and perhaps in the world. Escaped from the storm and from the fish, Jonah is once more called to warn the Ninevites. This time he obeys, and preaches to them with such success that they all repent and are forgiven. God is pleased, but Jonah is not; he is bitterly disappointed. He did not wish the Ninevites to be saved; he wished them to be lost. He supposed he had the congenial task of pronouncing doom upon the enemies of his people, and now it seemed that he had simply been opening the way for their repentance and God's forgiveness. He felt that he had been deceived and betrayed into giving his heathen enemies his own choicest and exclusive possession—the favor of God. No wonder Jonah is angry enough to die. But God rebukes him for his anger and bitterness, and declares his pity for the untold thousands of the great heathen city: "You had pity on the gourd, ... and should not I, indeed, have pity on Nineveh, that great city?"[5]

Nineveh had been the archenemy of the Jewish people, and it was asking a great deal to require Jonah to rejoice over its conversion and salvation. It was a hard lesson that the Book of Jonah sought to teach. But religion is something to be not hoarded but shared. Jonah is the first missionary book in the world. There's a wideness in God's mercy like the wideness of the sea, and the love of God is broader than the measure of man's mind. This is the imperishable truth of the Book of Jonah, and its unknown author cast it in such inimitable forms that his three-page story is among the masterpieces of the world.

The psalm in chapter 2 is a subsequent addition, in the latest Hebrew lyric style. It is manifestly in origin not a prayer for deliverance but a thanksgiving for a deliverance already accomplished.

SUGGESTIONS FOR STUDY

1. *References:* [1]Ezek. 33:11 (cf. 18:23); [2]Ezek. 18:31 (cf. 33:11); [3]II Kings 14:25; [4]Rom. 3:29; [5]Jonah 4:10, 11.

2. In what period is the scene of the story of Jonah laid?

3. Tell the story.

4. What did Nineveh stand for in Jewish experience?

5. How did the Jew feel about his relation to God?

6. How does the teaching of Jonah affect this?

7. What is its great religious lesson?

8. To what form of literature does the Book of Jonah belong?

CHAPTER XXI

THE SONG OF SONGS

Hebrew poetry was not all religious. The Hebrews were orientals and fully alive to the passionate appeals of existence. Their first literary expressions were war-songs and dirges.[1] The imprecatory psalms and the taunt-songs of the prophets show how they could hate, and their amorous impulses found full expression in one great love poem, the Song of Songs.

This form of title, like the King of Kings, or the Book of Books, means the greatest of songs. It was also called Solomon's Song, because Solomon was regarded as the greatest of the Hebrew song-writers; and so the greatest song would naturally be ascribed to him. He was said to have written five thousand songs.[2]

But the Song of Songs was not a product of court life, nor is it as ancient as the time of the undivided kingdom. It is in fact not a single song but a group of songs. Now it is the girl who sings, now it is her lover. They are village lovers, from some place not far from Jerusalem, as the references to scenes and places show. Each in turn gives utterance to the frankest and most passionate terms of affection.

It is still the custom in Syria for a bridal pair to

be treated as king and queen in their village during the week of the celebration of their marriage. The bridegroom is brought in state to the threshing floor where he is enthroned upon the threshing sledge with his bride, and hailed as king. The beauty of the bride is dwelt upon in great detail in the "wasf" or "description," and the passionate attachment of each for the other is described in the first person.

The significance of this for the Song is very clear. The bridegroom is called Solomon because Solomon was such a famous king, and he is "Solomon" for his week, in his village. And if he is Solomon, she is Shulammith,[3] which is clearly just a feminine form of the same name, as though he were called, as in Latin, Salomo, and she, Salome.

In chapters 4–7 at least we have such a series of songs, celebrating the beauty of the bride and the attractions of her lover, and hailing them as king and queen of the village:

> Ah, it is the litter of Solomon.
> Sixty warriors are around it,
>   of the warriors of Israel. . . . .
> O maidens of Jerusalem, go forth,
>   and gaze upon King Solomon.[4]

In fact, the whole Song is most naturally understood in this way. The bride and the bridegroom are represented as singing the solos and the villagers form the chorus. The bride exults in the affection of her lover, 1:2–4. The bride and bridegroom lavish compliments upon each other, 1:7—2:2. The bride declares to the villagers her devotion to him, 2:3—3:5. The chorus hails the bridegroom, enthroned on the threshing sledge, 3:6–11. The bridegroom rejoices in the beauty of the bride, 4:1–15. The bride declares the physical perfections of her lover, 5:10–16. The bridegroom returns the compliment, 6:4–10. As the bride dances the sword-dance the villagers dilate with the utmost frankness upon her charms, 6:13—7:6. The bridegroom and the bride, encouraged by the chorus, acknowledge the overwhelming power of love and their devotion to each other, 7:7—8:14.

We cannot be sure that the songs are in the order followed in such country weddings, but there is no serious reason for thinking they are not. The whole may at any rate be regarded as a little anthology of Hebrew wedding songs, rejoicing in the strong mutual attraction of the sexes culminating in happy and honorable marriage.

Efforts have been made to understand the Song as a little drama in six acts and twelve scenes, telling the story of a Shulamite girl brought to Solomon's court, but longing for her shepherd lover, with whom she is finally reunited. It would be gratifying to have even so small a fragment of Hebrew drama, but the explanation breaks down at too many points.

Others see in it a survival of the old nature-worship of Palestine, so denounced by the prophets. In the succession of the seasons this worship saw in the autumn the death of Tammuz and explained the spring as caused by his resurrection and marriage to the goddess Ishtar. In the Song, such interpreters say, Solomon was presently brought in and the goddess became the bride. This, too, is confused and difficult; the Song does not read in that way at all, though such old religious hymns may have influenced these songs.

The religious interpretations of the Song are also full of difficulty. Jewish thought has endeavored to see in it the union of God and his people, and Christian interpreters have understood it of Christ and the Church, or of Christ and the soul. When the bold oriental figures of which the Song is full are really understood, however, these fanciful religious interpretations are seen to be far-fetched and incongruous. Yet the Song is still publicly read among the Jews in celebration of the Passover.

The songs are, in fact, in their present form altogether wanting in religious feeling and interest. But it is a satisfaction to the student of Hebrew life and literature to have some of the purely secular poetry of the Hebrews, and the Song of Songs, with its rich oriental feeling and imagery, is all that we possess of that. It belongs late in Jewish history, probably in the fourth or the third century before

Christ, in the period of the Persian or the Greek domination.

1. *References:* [1]Judg., chap. 5; II Sam. 1:19–27; [2]I Kings 4:32; [3]Song of Songs 6:13; [4]Song of Songs 3:7, 11.

2. Name some varieties of Hebrew poetry.

3. To which of these does the Song of Songs belong?

4. What is the meaning of its name?

5. Why is it sometimes called Solomon's Song?

6. What are some modern interpretations of the Song?

7. What is the probable explanation of it?

8. How does this explain the use of the names Solomon and Shulammith?

9. Was Judaism an ascetic religion?

10. What is the literary value of the Song?

11. What place has the Song in modern Jewish practice?

CHAPTER XXII

THE BOOKS OF CHRONICLES, NEHEMIAH, AND EZRA

The conquests of Alexander left the Jewish community after his death subject to the Greek masters of Egypt, and no nearer than before to the independence and influence of which they dreamed. It was not strange that they found solace in these times of insignificance and humiliation in recalling the glories of the nation's past, and in repainting in glowing colors its departed splendors. The priesthood and the ritual had become more and more central and dominant in Jewish life. The priestly book of history and law had been written and its influence was at its height. It was natural that the nation's story, from the death of Saul to the reformation under Ezra, should be retold from the point of view of priestly standards and ideals.

It is this that is done in the books known to us as Chronicles, Ezra, and Nehemiah. They were originally a single continuous work, for the most part paralleling the narratives of II Samuel and I and II Kings. But here the colors are much deeper. Good kings are depicted as better, bad kings as worse, than in Samuel and Kings. Armies are larger, tribute is heavier—in general, figures and statistics are exaggerated. The priestly system and atmosphere are read back into the distant past. The Temple organization is credited to David in great detail, and all its appointments when it was erected under Solomon are dwelt upon at length, but the work of the prophets Elijah and Elisha is passed over in silence. The writer's interest is clearly in Temple and priesthood, and in the response of the kings to duties specifically religious.

II Kings stopped in the midst of the Exile, at the thirty-seventh year of the captivity of King Jehoiachin, or 561 B.C. But the Chronicler did not stop there. He went on with the decrees of Cyrus authorizing the Jews to return to their own land, and the work of Nehemiah and Ezra in reorganizing the emancipated Jews. For this part of his work he seems to have had further written sources, among them a very moving account by Nehemiah himself of his work,[1] and one Aramaic narrative from which he takes over short passages without translating them into Hebrew;[2] as though both languages would be equally intelligible to his readers.

He makes the work of Ezra precede that of Nehemiah, but careful modern study has established that Nehemiah's work began in 444 B.C. and Ezra's in 397 B.C., or perhaps even later. It is probable also that the humbler people who had never been carried into captivity played a larger part in rebuilding the city and Temple than the Chronicler indicates. In

Nehemiah,[3] the succession of high priests is brought down to Jaddua, whom Josephus mentions as high priest in the time of Alexander the Great.[4] The Chronicler's work must have been written soon after that time.

The vigorous stand of Ezra against intermarriage with foreigners is reflected in the Chronicler's great concern for unbroken Jewish genealogies, such as occupy chapters 1–8 of I Chronicles, and frequently intersperse the narrative, making the whole work a sort of Golden Book of Jewish ancestries. The scope of these genealogies—Adam, Seth, Enosh—shows that the writer knew not simply the books of Samuel and Kings but the great record of history and law known to us as Genesis to Joshua, indeed the whole historical literature of his people. His pious and priestly interest leads him to drop out of sight the recreant Northern Kingdom; he makes no effort to retell its story, and his interest in the Levites and his knowledge of Temple music make it clear that he himself is a Levite and a Temple musician.[5]

He re-writes the story of the kingdom of Judah not as Samuel and Kings had related it but on the understanding that the developed religious law of his own day had been in force through its whole history. His book is an imaginative priestly recast of Jewish history. It has been described as an ecclesiastical chronicle of Jerusalem.

To the historian the most convincing part of the

Chronicler's record is his picture of Nehemiah, and his coming to Jerusalem, surveying the ruined walls by night, and setting about their restoration. The first exiles to return had come back in 538 B.C., and began by building houses to live in. In 520, at the instance of Haggai and Zechariah, steps were taken to rebuild the Temple.[6] With Nehemiah, in 444, the walls are rebuilt.

But the condition of the people was still far from satisfactory from the new priestly point of view, and when Ezra the priest came in 397 B.C., or soon after, he called upon those who had married foreign wives to divorce them and cast off their children, for he looked upon such unions as pernicious and unclean.[7] This harsh position was sustained by the heads of families whom he called into conference on the matter, but it did not go unchallenged, as the Book of Ruth shows. Ezra represents the unflinching application of the priestly law to the people of Jerusalem, and the Chronicler reads back this law into all the previous history of the kingdom of Judah.

Sincere and high-minded as Ezra's purpose doubtless was in his reforms, they nevertheless tended to foster and establish in the Jewish mind those narrow ideals of legalism and exclusiveness that so blighted the subsequent course of Judaism, and have driven many of its best spirits, in ancient and modern times, out of its fellowship.

SUGGESTIONS FOR STUDY

1. *References:* [1]Neh. 2:11–20; [2]Ezra 4:7–23; 5:3—6:15; [3]Neh. 12:10 f.; [4]*Antiquities* xi. 7. 2; 8. 4; [5]I Chron., chaps. 24–26; II Chron. 5:12, 13; 35:15, etc.; [6]chap. xiii; [7]Ezra, chaps. 9, 10.

2. What period of Jewish history is covered by the books of Chronicles, Nehemiah, and Ezra?

3. What is the writer's distinctive point of view in writing?

4. What do we know of his position and interests?

5. How does he alter the picture given in Samuel and Kings? (Cf. I Kings 22:43 with II Chron. 17:6.)

6. What has he to say about the work of the prophets?

7. Why does he neglect the history of the Northern Kingdom?

8. What sources had he for the later period of Nehemiah and Ezra?

9. What was the work of Nehemiah?

10. What reforms did Ezra undertake?

11. What is the historical value of the books of Chronicles as compared with Samuel and Kings?

12. What was the writer's view of religion?

CHAPTER XXIII

THE BOOK OF LAMENTATIONS

Some of the earliest Hebrew poems that have come down to us are dirges. David composed one over Abner,[1] and a greater one over Saul and Jonathan:[2]

> "How have the heroes fallen! . . . .
> Swifter than eagles were they,
> They were stronger than lions. . . . .
> How have the mighty fallen,
> And the weapons of war perished!"

Amos sings a dirge over Israel:

> "Fallen, not to rise again,
>   is the virgin Israel;
> Prostrate on her own soil,
>   with none to raise her up."[3]

Amos wrote a generation before the fall of the Northern Kingdom, and a century and a half before the Babylonians took Jerusalem. The grief the Jews felt when the city was actually taken and the national life extinguished was far keener. It found expression in the dirges that form the main part of the Book of Lamentations.

Lamentations, or Dirges, consists of five poems, each forming a separate chapter in our modern versions. They deal with the misery of the conquered city and people. The first, second, and fourth of them are dirges lamenting the overthrow of Jerusalem as that of an individual, the daughter of Zion. The third is a lament over the writer's own sufferings, of course representing those of his people. The fifth is a prayer describing the misery and shame of the exiles.

The first four chapters are not only in the Hebrew elegiac meter, but are acrostic poems, the lines of each stanza beginning with the successive letters of the Hebrew alphabet. In chapters 1–3 these stanzas consist of three lines, but in chapter 4 of two. Strangely enough, in chapters 2, 3, and 4 the fifteenth and sixteenth letters of the Hebrew alphabet are transposed, but in chapter 1 they are in the conventional modern order. This suggests that these three poems are older than chapter 1, but the acrostic form of poetry was a late development of Hebrew literature and the whole book was written long after the events it so touchingly describes, probably some time in the third century before Christ.

The misery of the captured and pillaged city is movingly depicted in the first dirge:

How lonely the city sits,
    once so crowded with people! . . . .
Judah . . . . has to live among the nations,
    she can find no home; . . . .

The children are begging bread
    with none to offer it to them. . . . .
Better off are those stricken by the sword
    than those stricken by hunger. . . . .
No kings of the earth believed,
    nor any of the inhabitants of the world,
That the oppressor and enemy could enter
    the gates of Jerusalem.
It was for the sins of her prophets,
    the iniquities of her priests,
Who shed in her midst
    the blood of the righteous.[8]

When Jerusalem fell the Edomites who lived
southeast of Judah had joined in plundering them,
and this memory long rankled in the Jewish heart
and colors the closing stanzas of this dirge.[9]

The final chapter of Lamentations is a prayer for
God's mercy, and describes the sorrows of the exiles and their longing for home:

But thou, O Lord, art enthroned forever;
Thy throne endures from age to age. . . . .
Restore us, O Lord, to thyself, so that we may re-
    turn;
Renew our days as of old.[10]

These poems of lamentation bear witness to the
lasting impression made on the Jewish mind by the
Babylonian conquest and Exile. They show the Hebrew dirge in its most developed form, and consti-

tute the largest single group of acrostic poems in
Hebrew literature. Their especial concern for the
sufferings of children reflects a highly developed
sensibility. They were anciently ascribed to Jeremiah, but they present more contrasts than re-
semblances to his characteristic ideas and ways of
expression.

SUGGESTIONS FOR STUDY

1. *References:* [1]II Sam. 3:33, 34; [2]II Sam. 1:19–27;
[3]Amos 5:1, 2; [4]Lam. 1:1, 3, 11, 12; [5]Lam. 2:19; [6]Lam. 3:26–
28, 34–36; [7]Lam. 3:58, 59; [8]Lam. 4:4, 9, 12, 13; [9]Lam. 4:21,
22; [10]Lam. 5:19, 21.

2. To what type of Jewish literature do the Lamentations
belong?

3. What parts of the book do you find particularly moving?

4. Read David's dirge over Abner (II Sam. 3:33).

5. Read David's dirge over Saul and Jonathan (II Sam.
1:19–27).

6. With what national experience do the Lamentations
chiefly deal?

7. What is the central topic of Lamentations, chaps. 1, 2?

8. Who seems to be impersonated in the third poem?

9. Why are the Edomites so bitterly spoken of in chap. 4?

10. How many of these poems are in the acrostic style?

11. What other such poems does the Old Testament contain? (Cf. Nah., chap. 1; Prov., chap 31; Pss. 9–10, 25, 34,
37, 111, 112, 119, 145.)

12. What peculiarity in the order of the alphabet dis-
tinguishes chap. 1 from chaps. 2, 3, and 4?

13. Why were the Lamentations ascribed to Jeremiah?
Why was he called the Weeping Prophet?

CHAPTER XXIV
THE BOOK OF PROVERBS

Every people has its proverbs. They spring out of the wit and insight of the common people and can hardly be described as literary expressions. Their beauty lies in their brevity and detachment. Their life is not in books but on the lips of living men and women.

The Hebrews had such proverbs. But with them such detached aphorisms developed into a regular form of moral and even religious instruction. The proverb became a conscious, didactic method. Most proverbs are naïve instinctive expressions of homely, practical wisdom. But among the Hebrews the composing of proverbs was cultivated as an art.

The men who studied the writing of proverbs were the Wise Men, the Sages of Israel and in later times, under the Persian and Greek rule, they became the professional teachers of the Jewish youth. They would produce a whole series of proverbs, more or less connected, and embodying not simply worldly wisdom but religious ideas as well.

Sometimes they abandoned the brief proverb form and developed their thought into an extended poem usually in praise of Wisdom: the Appeal of

Wisdom, the Worth of Wisdom, the Blessings of Wisdom, the Invitation of Wisdom, Wisdom and Folly, and the like.[1] They also made it a practice to collect and edit proverbs, so that little books of them came into existence.

Studious and traveled men brought home from other lands foreign proverbs and put them into Hebrew, adapting them to Jewish ideas of God and religion. We have seen that after the Exile some Jews took refuge in Egypt, where they established a colony at Elephantine, near the First Cataract. Such refugees translated into Hebrew an old Egyptian work, the Wisdom of Amen-em-ope, which we know as Prov. 22:17—24:22. This ancient fragment of Egyptian Wisdom was probably composed some centuries before the Exile, long before the Jews had taken up the writing of proverbial literature, or Wisdom, and is the oldest part of the Proverbs.

The next oldest part of the book is the immediately preceding portion, 10:1—22:16, which probably comes from the Persian period, the fifth and fourth centuries before Christ. Chapters 1–9 are later, perhaps from the Ptolemaic times, especially the third century before Christ—which were more favorable to Jewish life.

The two main collections of independent proverbs in the book are 10:1—22:16, already mentioned, and chapters 25–29. The first of these, which is the oldest collection of native Hebrew proverbs, consists chiefly of simple two-line proverbs:

> Hope deferred makes the heart sick,
> But desire fulfilled is a tree of life.[2]

> A gentle answer turns away wrath,
> But harsh words stir up anger.[3]

In the second collection, chapters 25–29, the proverbs are often much longer, extending to four or even eight lines.

It is evident that the book is a collection of collections. Eight of these can be distinguished: 1–9; 10:1—22:16; 22:17—24:22 (the Words of the Wise); 24:23–34 (an appendix: further Words of the Wise); chapters 25–29 (the Proverbs of Solomon); chapter 30 (the Words of Agur); 31:1–9 (the Words of Lemuel); and 31:10–31 (the alphabetic poem on the Ideal Wife).

Nothing is known of Agur and Lemuel, but their connection with Massa points to Arabia as the reputed source of their wisdom. It is Agur who says "Give me neither poverty nor riches."[4] The final poem, on the Ideal Wife, reflects a higher position for Hebrew womanhood than was conceded her until long after the Exile. She is the symbol of thrift, industry, and foresight. "Her children rise up and bless her."[5]

The Sages have been called the humanists of Israel, and, like the greatest humanists, they were deeply religious. "The beginning of wisdom is reverence for the Lord" was the cornerstone of their work.[6] Our collection of Proverbs was probably completed in the third century before Christ, but it was followed in the second century by Ecclesiastes and the Wisdom of Jesus ben Sirach, and by the Book of the Wisdom of Solomon, who became the symbol of Wisdom not only to the Jews but to the Arabs. The authors of the Book of Kings said that his wisdom surpassed the wisdom of all the eastern Arabs and all the wisdom of Egypt, for he was wiser than all men, and uttered three thousand proverbs.[7] They came in this way to ascribe to him their proverbs just as they ascribed to David their psalms.[8]

The proverb is so portable a form of truth that it has always remained popular down to modern times, as the *Adages* of Erasmus and *Poor Richard's Almanac* show. And the division of the Bible into verse paragraphs in the sixteenth century has led most people to treat all its books as though they were made up of proverbs, each verse being considered an independent statement of truth. So the proverb style has dominated the use of the Bible, although properly it is confined to the Book of Proverbs.

SUGGESTIONS FOR STUDY

1. *References:* [1]Job, chap. 28; [2]Prov. 13:12; [3]Prov. 15:1; [4]Prov. 30:8; [5]Prov. 31:10–31; [6]Ps. 111:10; Prov. 9:10; [7]I Kings 4:30–32; [8]Prov. 1:1.

2. Repeat a few current proverbs.

3. What is the difference between such proverbs and those in the Book of Proverbs?

4. Who produced the proverbs?

5. What other books did they write?

6. Were all the proverbs of native Hebrew origin?

7. Through what stages of collection have they passed?

8. What are some of the most familiar ones?

9. Show how the proverb form grew among the Hebrews, from the simplest to the most developed kind.

10. When was our Book of Proverbs formed?

11. What kind of wife is described in the closing acrostic poem?

12. Is its form a mark of early or late date?

13. Does the ideal of womanhood it presents belong early or late in Hebrew development?

CHAPTER XXV

THE BOOK OF DANIEL

The efforts of the kings of Syria to impose Greek
ideals of life upon their subjects were strongly re-
sisted by the more pious Jewish groups, and when in
168 B.C. Antiochus Epiphanes, wishing his people to
have one civilization, proposed to obliterate everything that made the Jews different from the rest of
his subjects, the situation became desperate. The
observance of the Sabbath was forbidden, the Temple was plundered and desecrated, and Judaism was
outlawed.

Some Jews gave way before this systematic persecution and abandoned their religion. But the Pious,
as they were called—the Saints or Chasidhim—
would not give way. They refused to give up the
copies of their scriptures and endured martyrdom
rather than apostatize. At the little Judean town of
Modein where the Jews were commanded to attend
a heathen sacrifice, an old priest named Mattathias
and his sons killed the Syrian officer and broke up
the ceremony. This was the beginning of the Maccabean uprising, which was to emancipate Judea
from Syrian rule and make it once more for a time a
free and independent state.

The struggle was a hard one and must often have

seemed hopeless. But the Jews encouraged themselves with memories of the heroes of other days and
the difficulties they had surmounted. The chief of
these heroes was Daniel. He stood in Jewish legend
and tradition for the ideal exile, unflinchingly re-
solved to maintain the faith of his fathers at all
costs. In the intense heat of the Maccabean persecution these memories and traditions were cast into
the Book of Daniel.

The book consists of two parts. The first describes the experiences of Daniel and his three companions at the court of Nebuchadnezzar, chapters 1–
6. These noble young captives refuse to eat the unclean food of Babylon or to worship the idol set up
by the king. Daniel continues to pray to his God in
spite of the king's interdict. In short, the exiles do
just the things the Jews were forbidden by Antiochus to do, and God delivers them from the fearful
penalties thus incurred, the fiery furnace and the
lions' den. Daniel's wisdom stands out above that
of the heathen and Belshazzar's feast and Nebuchadnezzar's madness show in masterly dramatic
style what happens to kings who set themselves
against God.

The second part of Daniel, chapters 7–12, is a
series of four visions. They are in that apocalyptic
style which we have seen already in Zechariah and
Ezekiel. They set forth under the characteristic
apocalyptic symbolism the series of empires, Baby-

lonian, Persian, Greek, and Syrian, down to the
Maccabean time, when they are to end in destruction. The three and a half years[1] are the years between the termination of the Temple worship by
Antiochus and the resumption of Jewish worship
there under the Maccabees in 165.

The same meaning is conveyed by Nebuchadnezzar's dream, in chapter 2, where the different
parts of the statue represent the successive empires
that between Daniel's time and their own had ruled
the world. The last, the feet of iron and clay, is to
be broken into dust by the stone hewn without
hands from a mountain, which itself becomes a great
mountain that fills the earth.[2] This is the Kingdom
of God.

It was the habit of the later apocalyptists to describe the conditions of their own day under the
name of some great figure of antiquity, such as
Enoch, Seth, Noah, Adam, or Daniel, who is dramatically conceived as writing not for his own time
but solely for the far-off time to come: "Not for
this generation, but for a remote one which is for to
come," as the Book of Enoch puts it.[3] In the words
of the Book of Daniel, "It relates to the distant future."[4]

Daniel was evidently written in the midst of the
Maccabean struggle, between 168 and 165 B.C. The
"little horn" of chapter 8 is the persecuting Antiochus himself,[5] while chapter 11 reflects the contem-

porary history of the Syrian kingdom in its relations with Egypt and Rome in increasing detail until the "contemptible person" (Antiochus Epiphanes) makes his assault upon Judaism and the Temple worship.[6]

Daniel, like Ezra, is written partly in Hebrew and partly in Aramaic. When the Chaldean magicians are introduced in 2:4 they use the Aramaic language, which they might be expected to speak. But the book goes on in Aramaic to the end of the seventh chapter. After that it is Hebrew again. It is evident that when the book was written both Hebrew and Aramaic were familiar to Jewish readers.

The power and vigor of the imagery of Daniel and the strength of its religious faith have given it a high place both in literature and in religion. It served its immediate time by nerving the Maccabean party to resist the attack of their rulers upon the Jewish faith and to throw off the Syrian yoke.

SUGGESTIONS FOR STUDY

1. *References:* [1]Dan. 7:25; [2]Dan. 2:34, 44; [3]En. 1:2; [4]Dan. 8:26; [5]Dan. 8:9, 23–25;[6] Dan. 11:21.

2. What scenes in the Book of Daniel are most familiar to you?

3. To what type of literature does it belong?

4. What are some of the traits of that literature?

5. What situation led to the writing of Daniel?

6. How does it meet the situation?

7. Into what parts does the book fall?

8. What effect did it have upon the situation?

9. What other books of this kind did the Jews produce?

10. Has Daniel a religious lesson for us today, and if so what is it?

11. What literary value has the Book of Daniel?

12. Compare the visions of chaps. 7–12 with the visions of Zechariah.

13. Compare them with the visions of Ezekiel.

CHAPTER XXVI

THE BOOK OF PSALMS

Jewish religion expressed itself not only in laws and sermons but in hymns and prayers, and these were gathered up from time to time into collections, like our hymnbooks. Some of these are very old, going back to the time of the kingdom, and even perhaps to David himself. He was a poet, as his dirges over Abner and Saul show,[1] and Jewish tradition assigned to him almost half of its psalms. The second of the five books of psalms ends with the words, "The prayers of David the son of Jesse are ended,"[2] but eighteen other psalms are ascribed to David in the rest of the Psalter,[3] and the Septuagint or Greek translation of the Book of Psalms adds fifteen more. Thus the Hebrews did honor to their great hero by ascribing to him their choicest songs.

But the Psalter is for the most part the product of the age after the Exile, when the Temple worship became more and more the typical expression of Jewish religion. The older hymns were revised, just as ours have been, to accord with new attitudes and uses, and various collections were formed, some of which may still be distinguished in the Psalter. The psalms of the sons of Korah, 42–49, and those of the sons of Asaph, 73–83, were such collections. The former are spoken of in II Chronicles[4] as Levites who stood up to praise the Lord with an exceedingly loud voice. Asaph, too, was associated by the Chronicler with the ancient psalmody,[5] and was evidently one of the traditional founders of guilds of Temple singers.

Other collections visible within the present Psalter are the Songs of Ascents, 120–34, and the Hallelujah Psalms, 111–13, 146–50. The songs sung at the Passover—the Hallel—Pss. 113–18, also formed a unit in practical use; Pss. 113 and 114 were sung before the Passover supper and Pss. 115–18 after it; they were the "hymn" sung by Jesus and the disciples after the Last Supper.[6]

The presence of independent collections in the Psalter is shown by the duplicate psalms that it contains; Ps. 14 is identical with Ps. 53; Ps. 40:13–17 reappears as Ps. 70; Ps. 57:7–11 and Ps. 60:5–12 make up Ps. 108.

It is clear that our Psalter is a collection of collections—a grand collection that was to embrace them all, and so came to include a few duplicates. The Psalter was thus a growth, and reflects many periods and situations in Jewish religious life, from the kingdom down through the Exile and the second Temple to the times of the Maccabean struggle toward the middle of the second century before Christ. Its somewhat arbitrary division into five books reflects the earlier division of the Law into the five books of

The greatest of all antiphonies is Ps. 136. The great national experiences are mirrored and celebrated in the Psalter: exile, humiliation, persecution: Ps. 79 describes their distress when Antiochus made his attack upon their religion and worship:

> O God, the nations have come into thy inheritance;
> They have defiled thy holy temple;
> They have laid Jerusalem in ruins.[11]

Bitter memories of the Exile lingered in Ps. 137:

> By the rivers of Babylon,
> There we sat down, and wept, indeed,
> When we remembered Zion.[12]

Edom's malicious encouragement of the destruction of Jerusalem—

> "Raze it, raze it
> To its very foundations!"[13]

must not be forgotten, and the poet hopes in no chastened mood that the children of Babylon will in their turn be dashed to pieces on the rocks.[14] This is vengeful hatred, indeed, and may warn us nowadays not to indulge in hymns of hate.

The advance in Jewish thought toward a nobler and loftier conception of God is reflected in the psalms as is also the dawning consciousness of a great national religious mission, a messianic destiny.

It has been well said that the Psalter was not only the hymnbook but the prayer-book of the second Temple, and the chief modern interest in the psalms is as expressions of personal religious life—remorse, despair, repentance, communion, aspiration, faith, hope, assurance. The psalmist is now lonely in a strange land, now sick and discouraged:

> Out of the depths I cry to thee, O Lord.
> O Lord, hear my voice![15]

And the social value of religion is finely put in the lines:

> Lo, how good and lovely it is
> When brethren dwell together as one.[16]

It is the variety as well as the reality of these inward experiences that makes the psalms an inexhaustible treasure of religion. No one fathoms it all, because no one passes through all the trials it describes. For the psalms are the emotion of many hearts, the thought of many minds, most of them writing under great stress, and it is this deep and varied religious expression that makes the Psalter so universal in its appeal. Sometimes the writer's religion is of the Law and the Temple; he exults in his book of religion, as in Ps. 119, or finds gratification in the exercises of processional and liturgy. Sometimes it is as spiritual and free as anything in the prophets:

Sacrifice and offering thou dost not desire . . . .
Burnt offering and sin-offering thou dost not demand.[17]

Everyone has his favorite psalms, but the one of universal appeal is, of course, the Twenty-third, which stands unsurpassed and perhaps unequaled among the world's classics of devotion:

The Lord is my Shepherd; I shall not want.[18]

And no book in the Bible speaks more directly and widely to modern religious life than this wonderful old Hebrew hymnbook, which was so often revised and enlarged, and reached its present size probably about the middle of the second century before Christ, or soon after.

SUGGESTIONS FOR STUDY

1. *References:* [1]II Sam. 1:19–27; 3:33, 34; [2]Ps. 72:18; [3]Pss. 86, 101, 103, 108–10, 122, 124, 131, 133, 138–45; [4]II Chron. 20:19; [5]II Chron. 29:30; [6]Mark 14:26; [7]Ps. 122:1; [8]Ps. 24:3; [9]Ps. 24:4; [10]Ps. 68:24–26; [11]Ps. 79:1; [12]Ps. 137:1; [13]Ps. 137:7; [14]Ps. 137:9; [15]Ps. 130:1, 2; [16]Ps. 133:1; [17]Ps. 40:6; [18]Ps. 23:1.

2. What is the Psalter?

3. What can you say of its history?

4. What historical situations does it reflect?

5. What light does it throw upon Jewish religious practices?

6. What is the lesson of the imprecatory psalms?

7. What do the superscriptions deal with?

8. What light do the psalms throw upon Jewish personal religion?

9. What personal emotions find expression in the book?

10. What is the modern value of the psalms?

11. What are your favorite psalms?

12. When did the Jews sing psalms?

13. What influence have the psalms had upon Christian hymns?

authority is claimed for its institution. It was a purely secular expression of social Judaism.

That it was written long after the Persian Empire had gone out of existence is also shown by its picture of Persian court and official procedure, which is quite out of accord with what we learn of them from Persian sources. The book thus belongs with Ruth and Jonah as another Hebrew example of the short story, a kind of creative literature of which these three books form almost the beginning. Other Jewish examples are the books of Judith and Tobit in the Apocrypha. Ruth, Jonah, and Esther are all of them short stories with a purpose, though that of Esther is not religious but social. It is more developed in form than the others, and throws new light upon Hebrew literary genius. It belongs to the history of literature rather than of religion, and reminds us that the Old Testament gathers up the literary classics of one of the most gifted peoples of antiquity, which knew the uses not only of law, eloquence, history, and poetry but of fiction as well.

The Book of Esther in Hebrew is very generally given to Jewish boys nowadays, when they reach the age of thirteen, and often in the form of a manuscript roll, so that there are more manuscript copies of Esther in existence today than of any other book of the Old Testament.

SUGGESTIONS FOR STUDY

1. Is it wrong to write fiction?

2. What examples of fiction does Jewish literature contain?

3. What purpose controlled each of these books?

4. How does fiction differ from the work of the oriental story-teller?

5. What types of literature does the Old Testament contain?

6. What types does it lack?

7. Of the three short stories in the Old Testament, which exhibits the most artistic development?

8. What do the names Esther and Mordecai suggest as to the sources of the book?

9. What is the moral weakness of the book?

10. What is its moral strength?

CHAPTER XXVIII

THE BOOK OF ECCLESIASTES

The Greek name Ecclesiastes, meaning "Preacher," was intended as a translation of the mysterious name Koheleth under which the Book of Ecclesiastes was written. Koheleth, the son of David, who was king in Jerusalem,[1] was evidently a way of referring to Solomon, who was considered the wisest of men, and credited in I Kings[2] with an immense number of songs and proverbs.

The writer of Ecclesiastes looked at the facts of life and found no progress or satisfaction in them. They filled him with the most absolute despondency. Nature goes round and round in a purposeless routine (1:1–11):

> "All rivers run to the sea,
>   But the sea is never full. . . . .
>   There is nothing new under the sun."[3]

Learning, too, is a wretched business, and knowing wisdom and folly is simply striving for the wind (1:12–18):

> "For more wisdom is more worry,
>   And increase of knowledge is increase of sorrow."[4]

Indeed, all human effort seemed to him vain. The works of man are so evanescent, his life is so short!

Who can tell what use the future will make of his little accumulations of wisdom or property? "How the wise and the fool alike die! And I hated life, for everything that is done under the sun seemed to me wrong."[5]

Life offers no satisfaction and there is no after-life, declares Koheleth. It is all futility, as he repeatedly says. He is a thoroughgoing pessimist; at least he writes in a mood of utter pessimism. He doubtless lived in a time when religion seemed lifeless and perfunctory, when the pursuit of truth had not revealed its immense attraction for the human mind, and when men had not awakened to the social opportunity afforded by the sheer needs of their fellows. The Greek pursuit of beauty in art and architecture and of truth in philosophy and science had not reached this Jewish philosopher, and the undoubted narrowness, formalism, and complacency of later Jewish thought threw him back upon himself.

It seems quite obvious to us that the real basis of Koheleth's bleak pessimism is his own utter selfishness, and we wonder whether there was no suffering humanity to be helped and comforted in his day. If he had had any disposition to serve God or even his fellow-men, he might have found life full of the deepest satisfactions. And if everybody had approached life as he did, this would today be a much more backward and unlovely world than it is. In our desperate hours we sometimes cheer ourselves with thoughts of wise and good women: "Das ewig Weibliche zieht uns hinan." But even this was denied to Koheleth: "One man out of a thousand have I found, but not a woman have I found among all these."[6] He fully shared the Jewish undervaluation of women.

But his work was afterward embellished by another of the Wise Men of Israel, who sought to lighten its darkness with some of the shrewd practical aphorisms of the Sages, and to show that after all things are not as bad as Koheleth had represented them. Of course the literary effect of Koheleth's picture lay in his tremendous overstatement. He means to paint a very dark picture. But its very darkness makes every reader protest, and one of these ancient readers wrought into it the moderating touches mentioned above. When Koheleth laments that all the labor and all the hard work are due to men's jealousy of one another, the Sage pointedly observes, "The fool folds his hands and devours his own flesh."[7] When Koheleth bitterly cries, "For whom should I toil and deny myself happiness?"[8] the Sage remarks, "Two are better than one, for they get a good wage for their toil; and if they fall, the one can lift up his companion, but if a solitary person falls there is no partner to lift him up."[9] This is a keen hint of the social value of life and work much needed by Koheleth.

But Koheleth needed more than the frigid proverbs of the Wise Men to balance its unreligious bitterness. For while the author acknowledged the existence of God, it seems to have meant almost nothing to him religiously; it did not give him light or hope or courage. This must have been the feeling of the pious Jew who perhaps not many years after its appearance wrought into it those great statements of religion that so enrich and glorify it. When Koheleth told young men to make the most of life's enjoyments while they could, the new voice is heard saying, "But know that for all these things God will bring you into judgment."[10] And a little farther on, in the same poem on the fleeting joys of youth, he sternly interjects, "Remember your Creator in the days of your vigor,"[11] which seriously interrupts and contradicts the flow of Koheleth's words. To fear God and keep his commandments is the thing that most concerns every man, for God will bring every work into judgment.[12] This is the last word of the book, and it is clear that it sounds much more like his religious reviser than like world-weary, disillusioned old Koheleth.

The book was written about the end of the third century before Christ, or not far from 200 B.C. Of its literary power there can be no doubt. The concluding poem, 11:9—12:8, with its inimitable picture of old age and death, is one of the gems of biblical literature. But the book is full of memorable sayings:

"Cast your bread upon the surface of the water,
For after many days you will find it."[13]

It has been finely said that the three hands that
may be distinguished in Koheleth are just those
types of mind mentioned by Paul in I Corinthians[14]
—the scribe, the wise man, and the searcher of this
world. It was the last who wrote the book, and the
wise man and the scribe retouched it. It might be
called "The Three Voices." And when we come to
the last lines of it, we seem to hear each of them
speak in turn:

Furthermore, my son, take warning: of the making of many books there is no end, and much study
is weariness of the flesh.[15]

The words of the wise are like goads; but collections which are given by one teacher are like nails
driven with a sledge.[16]

The conclusion of the matter. Let us hear all:
Fear God and keep his commandments.[17]

It is well that they do all speak. For the modern
man too is faced with the uncompromising material
facts of science, which he must relate to culture and
religion in his turn. And so he can still find a lesson
in this strangest book in the Old Testament.

SUGGESTIONS FOR STUDY

1. *References:* [1]Eccles. 1:1; [2]I Kings 4:32; [3]Eccles. 1:7, 9;
[4]Eccles. 1:18; [5]Eccles. 2:16, 17; [6]Eccles. 7:28; [7]Eccles. 4:5;
[8]Eccles. 4:8; [9]Eccles. 4:9, 10; [10]Eccles. 11:9; [11]Eccles. 12:1;

[12]Eccles. 12:13; [13]Eccles. 11:1; [14]I Cor. 1:20; [15]Eccles. 12:12; [16]Eccles. 12:11; [17]Eccles. 12:13.

2. How are the conflicting statements and attitudes of Ecclesiastes explained?

3. When was it written?

4. What was the writer's general position?

5. What was done to it afterward?

6. To which of the hands that worked upon it would you assign 7:4–6? 7:7–12? 7:19? 10:1–3? 8:14a?

7. Who is meant by Koheleth?

8. Why was the book ascribed to him?

9. Why do we call the book Ecclesiastes?

10. Does anyone today maintain the position taken in the original body of the book?

11. What is the religious answer to that position?

12. How would you distribute the last three verses of the book among the three hands that have worked upon it?

CHAPTER XXIX

THE FORMATION OF THE OLD TESTAMENT

The works of Hebrew literature have come down to us assembled into a collection which we know as the Old Testament. This collection was gradually formed by the Jews for their own religious purposes, but they did not of course call it the Old Testament. They called it the Scriptures, or the Law and the Prophets, or simply the Law. How did it originate, and through what stages did it pass?

The beginning of the Old Testament was the finding of the book of Deuteronomy in the Temple in 621 B.C. That book became the nucleus of the Jewish scriptures. It was gradually expanded through the addition of the prophetic history in the course of the sixth century, only the legal parts of the whole being regarded as authoritative.

When Ezra the priest soon after 400 B.C. stood up before the people and read the Book of the Law aloud to them day after day, it marked not only the introduction of the Synagogue into Palestine, but also a new step in the progress of the Jewish scripture, for the Law he read was probably the new priestly recast of Hebrew history and legislation.[1] This was itself soon combined with the expanded Deuteronomy into our Hexateuch—Genesis, Exo-

dus, Leviticus, Numbers, Deuteronomy, Joshua.
But since the Law stopped with Deuteronomy,
Joshua naturally fell away, and the Pentateuch, or
work of five books remained.

The harsh measures of Nehemiah and Ezra in de-
manding that marriages with foreign women be an-
nulled met with much opposition. One son of the
high priest refused to give up his foreign wife, the
daughter of Sanballat the Horonite,[2] and was ex-
pelled. Sanballat built him a temple on Mount
Gerizim, near Shechem, and the Samaritan church
was the result. These Samaritans have always cherished the Law—the five books of Moses, and no
more—and they possess to this day a Samaritan
manuscript of it for which they claim a great antiquity. This shows that when they broke off from the
Jews of Jerusalem the Jewish scripture had reached
that stage but no further.

While this Samaritan schism began about 432
B.C., the breach with the Jerusalem community did
not at once become complete. Still we may be sure
the acceptance by both Jerusalem and Samaria of
the completed Genesis to Deuteronomy must have
taken place by the middle of the following century.
The advocates of the priestly book of law and history would naturally seek to have it combined with
the expanded Deuteronomy which contained the
nation's law, and this must have happened soon
after Ezra's appearance with the priestly book, in

397 B.C. In fact, he may have been active in securing their amalgamation.

With Joshua the books of Judges, Samuel, and Kings were presently grouped, under the title of the Former Prophets. The Jews had begun to collect the works of the literary or writing prophets in the time of the Exile, so that a collection of these Latter Prophets also was already well advanced. The prophetic collection as a whole, including both Former and Latter Prophets, came to be recognized as authoritative between 250 and 175 B.C., for the Chronicler evidently did not regard the Former Prophets as scripture, or he could not have reshaped them so freely into the books of Chronicles. Jesus, son of Sirach, on the other hand, who about 180 B.C. composed his Wisdom, our Ecclesiasticus, in Jerusalem, spoke of the Law, the Prophets, and the rest of the books as making up the sacred writings of his people; at least that expression occurs more than once in the Greek translation of his book made by his grandson at Alexandria about 132 B.C. The collection of the prophets was clearly accepted in their days.

The Latter Prophets included Isaiah, Jeremiah, Ezekiel, and the Book of the Twelve, which we know as the Minor Prophets, Hosea to Malachi. But it was counted as one book by the Jews. This made the number of the Latter Prophets the same as that of the Former, that is, four.

The books of the prophets did not, however, stand on quite the same level of authority as the books of the Law. The prophets were subordinated to the Law, and in many ways discriminated from them in prestige. In these later days of Judaism the priestly had thus prevailed over the prophetic element in final influence.

The Psalms formed the nucleus of the third group of sacred books. They are quoted as scripture in I Maccabees, written probably early in the first century before Christ. With them were associated Job and Proverbs. The Five Rolls also came into this last division of Hebrew scripture: The Song of Songs, Ruth, Lamentations, Ecclesiastes, and Esther, each of which was read at one of the five religious festivals of the Jewish year, from Passover to Purim.

The last group in this part of the scripture was formed by Daniel, Ezra-Nehemiah, and Chronicles, making a total, as the Jews counted, of twenty-four books, corresponding to the number of letters in the Hebrew alphabet, which may be reckoned as either twenty-two or twenty-four.

The Hebrew scripture did not reach these final proportions until the end of the first century after Christ, however, for uncertainty was felt as to the Song of Songs and Ecclesiastes until the synod of Jamnia, about the end of the first century after Christ, and even after that some rabbis did not accept Esther as a book of scripture.

Lessons both from the Law and from the prophets were read in the synagogue every Sabbath in New Testament times, but it must be remembered that in Jewish regard the Law was supreme over both Prophets and Writings.

The theory on which the decision as to the canonicity of doubtful books was reached was that the prophetic period had extended from Moses to Ezra, and that books falling within that period might properly be accepted. Proverbs, Ecclesiastes, and the Song of Songs purported to be the works of Solomon; the Psalms, of David; Esther and Daniel dealt with scenes and persons of the fifth and sixth centuries before Christ. There was, therefore, some color for admitting these books to the Jewish scripture as belonging to the times before Ezra (397 B.C.). This rabbinical conception of a definite prophetic period to which a book must belong if it was to be considered scripture is the key to the last stage in the development of the Old Testament.

SUGGESTIONS FOR STUDY

1. *References:* [1]This is indicated by the fact that the people in response to his efforts kept the Feast of Booths for eight days, as the new priestly law required, not for seven, as the older Deuteronomy provided; Neh. 8:14–18; Lev. 23:36; Deut. 16:13; [2]Neh. 13:28; Josephus, *Antiquities* xi. 7.2; 8.4.

2. What is the source of our Old Testament?

3. What book may be regarded as the nucleus of the collection?

4. Into what did this book develop?

5. What was the book from which Ezra the priest read before the people in 397 B.C.?

6. What became of this book?

7. How did the Samaritan community arise, and what is its scripture?

8. What is meant by the Former Prophets?

9. What constituted the Latter Prophets?

10. When were these collections combined into the Prophets?

11. What religious use was made of the Law and the Prophets?

12. What was the third part of the Hebrew scriptures?

13. What three groups did it contain?

14. What liturgical use was made of some of these?

15. About what books was there most uncertainty?

16. How was it terminated?

17. What is meant by the prophetic period, and how did it affect the problem?

CHAPTER XXX

THE APOCRYPHAL BOOKS

The Hebrews produced many other books besides those preserved in our Bible. Some of these are mentioned in the Old Testament, but have long since disappeared: the Book of Jashar;[1] the Book of the Chronicles of the Kings of Judah;[2] the Book of the Chronicles of the Kings of Israel.[3] In general, the Old Testament (aside from Esther and the Song of Songs) contains only the religious literature of Judaism and by no means all of that.

Of the lost books of Hebrew literature some were fortunately translated into Greek and have survived in that language. The Bible of early Christianity was the Greek translation of the Jewish scriptures, which included some of these books now lost in Hebrew, as well as others that were originally written in Greek. When toward the close of the fourth century after Christ Jerome set about revising the Old Latin Bible, he tried to find the Hebrew originals of all the Old Testament books to help him in his task, and the books of which he could find no Hebrew copies he set apart in a group by themselves and named the Apocrypha, the Secret Books or Books of Hidden Wisdom. As the first English Bible in its Old Testament portion was translated from the Latin (Coverdale, 1535), the

Apocrypha passed into the English Bible, and they still find a place in all complete printings of the King James Version, of 1611. Though they are in general from a rather late period, they contain much of literary and historical interest, and some passages of real religious value.

The Book of Tobit tells the story of a pious Jew whose steadfast devotion to alms, prayer, tithes, and the observance of the Law was, after a bitter experience of blindness, poverty, and humiliation, finally rewarded. The main episode is the journey of his son Tobias from Nineveh to recover a sum of money previously deposited by Tobit with a friend in Rages. Tobias is accompanied on the journey by the angel Raphael disguised as a guide or dragoman. At Ecbatana, Tobias meets his cousin Sarah and falls in love with her. She had been given to seven husbands in succession, but each of them had been killed on the wedding night by the demon Asmodeus, who loved her. With the aid of Raphael, Tobias routs the demon, the money is brought from Rages, and on their joyful return to Nineveh, Tobit's sight is restored.

The book is a piece of religious fiction, almost a fairy story, written probably in Greek, and in Egypt, where it may have been intended as an answer to a local production, the Tractate of Khons, which was designed to promote the worship of that Egyptian deity, and told how with the aid of Khons a demon was cast out of a princess. The popular Jewish Story of the Wise Ahikar is also reflected. Tobit was written probably between 190 and 175 B.C., and gives a faithful picture of Jewish ideals of piety at that time, in devotion to the Law and the Temple. The appearance of angels and demons—Raphael, one of the seven archangels,[4] and Asmodeus, the evil demon[5]—is a definite development in Jewish ideas, under Persian influence, which was later to play an important part in New Testament times.

The longest of the Apocrypha is the Wisdom of Jesus, the son of Sirach. It is a typical piece of Jewish Wisdom Literature, like Proverbs. It was written by a Jewish scribe of Jerusalem before the outbreak of the Maccabean struggle, and probably about 180 B.C. It was translated into Greek by the author's grandson on a visit to Alexandria about 130 B.C., for the translator states that he had come to Egypt in the thirty-eighth year of King Euergetes, or 132 B.C. The statement of the book that it is a translation has been confirmed in recent years by the discovery of about two-thirds of it in Hebrew manuscripts of the tenth or eleventh century after Christ, which were found in the storeroom of an old synagogue in Cairo, between 1896 and 1900. It is evident that it was in existence in Hebrew in Jerome's day, although he did not succeed in finding it.

The strength and the weakness of the scribal Judaism that began with Ezra are plainly seen in Ecclesiasticus, as the Greeks called the book. His conception of woman is absurdly low; a daughter is to him only an unending source of anxiety.[6] Yet his appreciation of the physician, the scribe, and especially the craftsman[7] is full of understanding. It is of the farmer, the jeweler, the smith, and the potter that he says: "They will maintain the fabric of the world. and in the handiwork of their craft is their prayer."[8]

The closing part of the book is a grand review of the great men of Jewish religious history, ending with Simeon the high priest, who died in 199 B.C. and was evidently a contemporary of the author, who pronounces a splendid eulogy upon him.[9] This review is introduced with the lines in praise of famous men,[10] which is the most quoted passage in all the Apocrypha: "Let us now praise famous men, our fathers before us."

The Greek form of the Book of Daniel contains various additions unknown to the Hebrew, which appear in the Apocrypha of the English Bible. The Prayer of Azariah and the Song of the Three Children are associated with the deliverance of Daniel's three friends from the fiery furnace. Both are pieces of Jewish liturgy—the Prayer from the dark days just before the Maccabean uprising, or about 170 B.C.; the Song a splendid psalm of thanksgiving, from the days of the Maccabean triumph, about 150 B.C.

In Bel and the Dragon, Daniel seeks to convince the king of Babylon of the falsity of his gods. To prove that the image of Bel does not eat the food left in his temple, Daniel has wood-ashes scattered on the floor, to record the footprints of the priests who come in the night to eat the offerings. And the Dragon, or serpent, which the king worships, Daniel kills by feeding him pitch and hair. The story was written to ridicule idolatry, probably in Greek about 100 B.C., when serpents were venerated in oriental and Greek shrines, like that of Aesculapius at Epidaurus.

The Story of Susanna reflects the efforts of the Pharisees in the first century before Christ to reform Jewish legal procedure in the matter of false witness to a capital charge. With many willing to act as informers, two might easily agree and condemn an innocent person to death. If they failed and were themselves convicted, they could not be executed, as no one had actually suffered. The remedy so dramatically urged in the Story of Susanna is twofold: the witnesses must be separately examined; and if their testimony is shown to be false they must be executed, whether the person they have accused has been put to death or not. The Story was probably written in the first quarter of the first century before Christ, in Jerusalem, by some Pharisee, and perhaps in Hebrew, although Julius Africanus, the friend of Origen, offered strong arguments for a Greek original.

The Book of Judith is the romantic account of how a beautiful Jewish woman named Judith, when her town was besieged by an Assyrian army under Holofernes, penetrated into the Assyrian camp, captivated Holofernes, and beheaded him in his sleep, thus delivering her city from its danger. Its purpose is to bring home to its readers the necessity of strict observance of the Jewish Law. In all the exacting situations in which Judith finds herself, she scrupulously observes the fasts, feasts, food laws and ablutions prescribed by the Law, and so earnestly insisted upon by the Pharisees. It is a significant document of Pharisaism.

Judith is extant in a short Hebrew form in a manuscript of the tenth century, and in a much-expanded Greek revision. It was composed probably about 150 B.C., when the Pharisaic movement began to develop actively after the Maccabean struggle, and it assumed its fuller Greek form about a century later.

The book is another example of Jewish religious fiction. The author seems almost to advertise the unhistorical character of his work by his opening statement that Nebuchadnezzar "reigned over the Assyrians in Nineveh." Nebuchadnezzar was the king of the Babylonians and his capital was Babylon, not Nineveh, as every Jew would know, for it was he that had captured and destroyed Jerusalem and carried the Jews to captivity in Babylon. The historical value of Judith lies in its picture of early

Pharisaism, not in any light it might cast upon the reign of Nebuchadnezzar, and its undoubted literary power and interest have given it an enduring place in the world's literature.

The supplementary chapters of Esther appear in the King James Bible as 10:4—16:24, but they appear in the Greek version of Esther scattered through the book. In general they seek to give to the book the religious tone it so manifestly lacks. They were probably introduced into it sometime between 150 and 100 B.C.

I Esdras is in the main an imaginative account, probably of Greek origin, of the rebuilding of the Temple. It tells the story of the three guardsmen of Darius and their answers to the question, "What is strongest?" One said wine, another, the king; and the third, woman, though truth was mightiest of all. He was adjudged the victor, and chose as his reward the rebuilding of the Temple.

The story was written not long after 150 B.C., probably in Alexandria. Its historical value is slight, but its literary interest is considerable. From it comes the famous proverb, "Truth is mighty and will prevail."[12]

II Esdras, in the English Apocrypha, consists chiefly of a series of apocalyptic visions from different hands, composed for the most part late in the first or early in the second century after Christ.

The Prayer of Manasseh is not really a part of the

Greek version of the Old Testament, but stands in a very few manuscripts with other materials at the end of the Psalms. It is a fine prayer of penitence, of Pharisaic color, and was written, probably in Greek, in the first half of the first century before Christ, 100–50 B.C. It was later identified with the prayer said in II Chronicles[13] to have been uttered by the wicked king Manasseh in his distress, and so found its way into some Greek Bibles.

There are four books called Maccabees. I Maccabees is an account of the Maccabean struggle against the persecution of Antiochus Epiphanes, resulting in the rise of the Hasmoneans. It covers the period 175–132 B.C., and was written by a Jew of Palestine perhaps half a century after the latter date. It was written in Hebrew or Aramaic, but was soon translated into Greek, in which form alone it survived. It is an important and generally trustworthy source for the history of its time.

II Maccabees, on the other hand, was written in Greek, and deals in a rhetorical and somewhat fanciful way with the stirring events of 175–160 B.C. It was probably composed in Alexandria, and has no such claims to historical worth as has I Maccabees. But its language influenced the writer of the Epistle to the Hebrews.[14]

III Maccabees is a romantic story of the effort of Ptolemy Philopator to enter the Holy of Holies in Jerusalem. The priests refused to permit this, and he determined to take vengeance upon the Jews of Alexandria. Being providentially prevented, however, he became their protector and patron instead. The book was written in Greek, probably in the first century before Christ.

IV Maccabees is really a discussion of the control of the emotions by reason. The author is a man of Pharisaic and Stoic leanings. Much of his book is occupied by a panegyric upon the Maccabean martyrs. The book was written in Greek, probably early in the first century after Christ.

The Wisdom of Solomon is the work of two authors, the second beginning at 11:2 and continuing to the end. It was written in Greek probably in the latter half of the first century before Christ, for Egyptian Jews, to safeguard them against the perils of skepticism, materialism, idolatry, and persecution. It was well known to more than one New Testament writer—Paul,[15] the authors of Hebrews[16] and Ephesians.[17] It has been called the finest work of Alexandrian Judaism before the time of Christ. It was so congenial to early Christian thought that it was actually included in the earliest list of New Testament books that has come down to us, the Muratorian List, made up probably at Rome, about A.D. 200. To Wisdom we owe the beautiful line, "The souls of the righteous are in the hand of God."[18]

The Book of Baruch represents itself as written

by Jeremiah's friend Baruch in the fifth year after the destruction of Jerusalem by the Babylonians, or 582 B.C., and sent to Jerusalem with a sum of money to help support the cultus there—to buy burnt offerings and sin-offerings and incense,[19] though how this could be done, with the Temple in ruins and the priesthood scattered, is by no means clear. The book is chiefly of a liturgical character, and reflects not only II Maccabees and the ancient Jewish liturgy, but probably the fall of Jerusalem before the Romans in A.D. 70, when Jewish thought would naturally turn back to the similar experience of the Jewish people centuries before. The first section (1:1—3:8) is devoted to the praise of God, the confession of sin, and a prayer for God's mercy. The second (3:9—4:4) revives the counsels of the Sages: Wisdom is what is needed. The third (4:5—5:9) consists of two odes of comfort and cheer, reflecting the later part of Isaiah and the Psalms of Solomon (ca. 50 B.C.). The sixth chapter is the so-called Letter of Jeremiah, which seeks to keep the Jews from falling into idolatry. The work as a whole belongs to the end of the first or the beginning of the second century after Christ.

Other Jewish books, like the apocalyptic Book of Enoch (second century B.C.), and the Psalms of Solomon, or Psalms of the Pharisees (first century B.C.), were known and read in Greek by the early Christians. Indeed, it is difficult to set definite limits to the collection of books they admitted to their Old Testament as sacred scripture. But the firm hand of Jerome drew a line between the books extant in Hebrew and accepted by the Jews of Palestine and the books known to him only in Greek, and ruled the former only in the full sense canonical and authoritative, and in this most Protestant churches have followed him.

SUGGESTIONS FOR STUDY

1. *References:* [1]Josh. 10:13; II Sam. 1:18; [2]I Kings 22:45; [3]I Kings 22:39; [4]Tob. 12:15; [5]Tob. 3:8; [6]Ecclus., chap. 42; [7]Ecclus., chap. 38; [8]Ecclus. 38:34; [9]Ecclus., chap. 50; [10]Ecclus., chap. 44; [11]Judith 1:1; [12]I Esd. 4:41; [13]II Chron. 33:12, 13; [14]Heb. 11:35 (cf. II Macc. 6:19, 30); [15]Rom. 9:21–23; [16]Heb. 1:3; [17]Eph. 6:11–20; [18]Wisd. 3:1; [19]Baruch 1:10.

2. What books mentioned in the Old Testament have disappeared?

3. What circumstance has preserved many books now lost in Hebrew?

4. How did these books come to be called the Apocrypha?

5. How did they happen to find a place in the first English Bibles?

6. What is the story of Tobit?

7. When was it written and why?

8. When was Ecclesiasticus written and by whom?

9. What are some of its values?

10. What is the significance of the Story of Susanna?

11. What was the purpose of "Bel and the Dragon"?

12. What is the story of Judith, and what was its purpose?

13. What was the purpose of the Greek additions to Esther?

14. What is the story of the Three Guardsmen?

15. What is the historical value of I Maccabees, and what period does it cover?

16. Characterize the other books of Maccabees.

17. What were the date and purpose of the Wisdom of Solomon?

18. What is the character of the Book of Baruch and when was it written?

19. Do you think these books should be included in the Old Testament, as they are in Greek Bible and the King James Version, or omitted from it, as they were by the Palestinian Jews and the Puritans?

CHRONOLOGICAL SURVEY

B.C.

Ca.	1150	The Song of Deborah
Ca.	850	The Judean History
	765–750	The work of Amos
Ca.	750	The Ephraimitic History
	745–735	The work of Hosea
	730–721	The work of Micah
	740–701	The work of Isaiah
	721	The Fall of Samaria
By	650	The Judean and Ephraimitic Histories combined
Ca.	650	The Book of Deuteronomy
	627	The Scythian Invasion; Zephaniah
	621	The Finding of Deuteronomy
	612	The Fall of Nineveh; Nahum
	608–597	The work of Habakkuk
	627–586	The work of Jeremiah
	597	The Fall of Jerusalem
	597–538	The Exile
	592	The Call of Ezekiel
	586	The Second Capture of Jerusalem
	586–538	The Histories combined with Deuteronomy
	550	The book of Samuel-Kings completed
	538	The Fall of Babylon; the return from Exile; Isa., chaps. 40–55
	520–519	The work of Haggai and Zechariah
Ca.	475–450	The work of Malachi
	444	The work of Nehemiah
Before	400	The Book of Obadiah
		The priestly book of law and history
		The Book of Judges completed

B.C.

Ca.	400	The Book of Joel
Ca.	397	The work of Ezra
Ca.	350	The formation of the Hexateuch
Before	300	The work of the Chronicler
	300–200	The books of Lamentations and Proverbs
Ca.	165	The Book of Daniel
	200–150	The Book of Ecclesiastes
Ca.	150	The completion of the Psalter
Ca.	150	The Book of Esther

BIBLIOGRAPHY

GENERAL

MOORE, G. F. *The Literature of the Old Testament.* New York: Holt, 1913.

BOX, G. H. *A Short Introduction to the Literature of the Old Testament.* London: Rivingtons, 1909.

GRAY, G. B. *A Critical Introduction to the Old Testament.* New York: Scribner, 1913.

FOWLER, H. T. *A History of the Literature of Ancient Israel from the Earliest Times to 135 B.C.* New York: Macmillan, 1922.

BEWER, J. A. *The Literature of the Old Testament in Its Historical Development.* New York: Columbia University Press, 1922.

CORNILL, G. H. *A Short Introduction to the Canonical Books of the Old Testament.* New York: Putnam, 1907.

DRIVER, S. R. *An Introduction to the Literature of the Old Testament.* Rev. ed. New York: Scribner, 1913.

CREELMAN, H. *Introduction to the Old Testament, Chronologically Arranged.* New York: Macmillan, 1917.

OESTERLEY, W. O. E. *The Books of the Apocrypha, Their Origin, Teaching and Contents.* New York: Revell, 1914.

TRANSLATIONS

The Bible: An American Translation. Edited by J. M. POWIS SMITH and EDGAR J. GOODSPEED. Chicago: University of Chicago Press, 1931.

The Holy Bible: A New Translation. By JAMES MOFFATT. New York: Doran, 1926.

The Holy Scriptures according to the Masoretic Text: A New Translation. By MAX L. MARGOLIS and OTHERS. Jewish Publication Society, 1917.

INDEX

[PRINTED IN U·S·A·]